VEGETARIAN Express Lane Cookbook

Vegetarian Express Lane Cookbook

Hassle-Free, Healthful Meals for *Really* Busy Cooks

Sarah Fritschner

Illustrations by Lingta Kung

Houghton Mifflin Company
Boston New York

Library of Congress Cataloging-in-Publication Data

Fritschner, Sarah.

Vegetarian express lane cookbook : hassle-free, healthful meals for really busy cooks / Sarah Fritschner; illustrations by Lingta Kung.

p. cm.

Includes index.

ISBN 0-395-97175-6

1. Vegetarian cookery. 2. Quick and easy cookery. I. Title.

TX837.F7356 1996

641.5'636—dc20 95-53975

CIP

Printed and bound in Canada by Best Book Manufacturers Inc.
Louiseville, Quebec

10 9 8 7 6 5 4 3 2 1

Designed by Susan McClellan and Eugenie Seidenberg Delaney

Contents

Introduction

Cooking family meals sometimes seems like a relentless job with an impossible mandate: to please all the people all the time on a budget, with at least a perfunctory attempt at good nutrition—all on a tight schedule. Most family cooks do this job every day—or aim to—under severe time and energy limitations. After a whole day at work, whether inside or outside the home, it's doubly difficult to get creative, to adapt to changing tastes of diners, to balance a meal.

So why would any cook add more restrictions to the job by eliminating meat, fish and poultry from dinner menus?

Let's see, could it possibly be because home-fried potatoes with feta cheese and black olives tastes a whole lot better than a skinless, boneless chicken breast? Could it be that black bean chili is less messy to make and just as satisfying as chili with meat? Or perhaps it is because we now know that our diet becomes immeasurably more balanced when we have greens and rice more often than pork chops.

In fact, vegetarian dishes are mainstays among many of the world's greatest cuisines.

Ask any native of Italy, Morocco or India—just to name a few—to name some favorite foods and you'll likely hear the simplest combinations in reply. Those mothers were as busy as we are and didn't spend all day at the kitchen stove. A Greek friend mentions spaghetti with fresh parsley, olive oil and lots of fresh lemon. A Sicilian I know serves fancy Italian food in his restaurant but prefers to eat a humble vegetarian dish of noodles with cauliflower and currants at his own table. One of the most beloved dishes of a Spanish couple up the street is a creamy omelet stuffed with potatoes and draped with broiled green peppers.

ONCE I CLOSED the door on meat dependence, a world of possibilities opened. Had I been stuck on grilled chicken, I would never have discovered spicy chick-peas with creamy tomato gravy. Had I been inextricably committed to ham, I would never have served black bean chili at my wedding reception. Had I planned to bring a sausage casserole to a Kentucky Derby Day brunch, I never would have become known for my savory phyllo-wrapped spinach pie, which has now become the focus of my Christmas Eve dinner as well.

But just because I like Moroccan couscous or Chinese stir-fries doesn't mean I can spend all day traveling around to a bunch of specialty shops or trying to perfect foreign cooking techniques. As an average cook in an average home with an average family, I can tell you one thing I am *not* doing is stopping on the way home from work to pick up fermented black bean paste. I want the food quick, with little cleanup, and I absolutely require one-stop shopping. If I can't pick it up when I stop for milk, it isn't dinner.

So I shop at the nearby supermarket, which does not carry sun-dried tomatoes, hoisin sauce or porcini mushrooms—ingredients that undoubtedly make vegetarian food taste fabulous. But my supermarket does carry many other foods that make great, quick vegetarian dinners: dried noodles, rice, fresh fruits and vegetables, milk, cheeses, pickles, bread, dried spices and sometimes fresh herbs and a growing variety of ethnic foods.

These ordinary ingredients are the ones called for in the recipes in this book. The dishes here don't require lots of preparation time, don't have lots of unnecessary calories and don't cost an arm and a leg.

For me, as for many other cooks, the most difficult part of the family meal is not shopping but planning. For this reason, I have arranged the recipes in chapters titled "Beans," "Rice,"

"Pasta" and "Pizzas," so you can turn right to the category that includes the kind of main dish you want.

You may notice, though, that there aren't any recipes containing tofu and meat analogs made from soybeans, which used to be cornerstones of vegetarian cooking in this country. That's because I think tofu tastes best in Asian food—and my stove is pathetically weak in BTUs to produce the great tofu-containing dishes of China. And I don't think tofu and other soybean products add enough flavor to other vegetarian dishes to make them worthwhile.

NONVEGETARIANS OFTEN WORRY that people who don't eat meat won't get enough protein or will suffer from other vitamin deficiencies. But luckily, a healthful vegetarian diet is just as easy as a healthful diet with meat—perhaps easier. Americans already get twice as much protein as they need, and some researchers think too much can cause some people to excrete calcium, leading to brittle bones. In addition, red-meat diets are believed to contribute to heart attacks.

When you become a vegetarian, your health considerations shift. Instead of concentrating on reducing fat, calories and protein, you should focus on getting enough calcium, iron, B_{12} and zinc. Greens, broccoli, okra, sesame seeds and almonds are all sources of calcium, and beans, grains and vegetables can give you all the iron and zinc you need. If you eat eggs, milk, cheese, yogurt or fortified breakfast cereal, B_{12} will be no problem.

TAKING THE FIRST STEP toward vegetarian cooking doesn't usually happen all at once. It often starts with just one dish that helps you become more confident—and more curious. With my friend, who considers herself the archetypal noncook, it was Kale and Currants (page 158), which she tried against her better judgment. She had always hated kale because she grew up eating it badly prepared. Now she cooks it often, and I've even heard her boast, "I have a great recipe for kale." My friend still doesn't consider herself a cook and she isn't a vegetarian, but she now feels more adept at putting good-tasting, nutritious, inexpensive food on the family dinner table.

Who can ask for more than that?

Catching the Flavor Express

VEGETARIAN FOOD can delight and satisfy even without lengthy preparation procedures. These are some ways I've found to decrease the time I spend on dinner while increasing the flavor:

- Don't overplan. If you're serving three different dishes, you don't want to spend time and creative energy on each one. A standard meal in my family is Ginger-Roasted Green Beans (page 156) served with plain rice and applesauce from a jar. I've exerted a little effort on the beans, virtually none on the other two. If you're tossing a salad—washing, drying and tearing lettuce leaves, preparing dressing and maybe some other additions—keep the rest of the choices simple: a baked potato and roasted carrots (both can cook in the oven at the same time), or sweet potato disks and garlic bread.

- Use wide pans. They have more surface area, so the food cooks faster. Since moisture evaporates more quickly, sauces will thicken faster too. My favorite pan is a 12-inch skillet with straight sides.

- For more taste, roast vegetables. Just as roasted meat gets flavor from its brown coating, so vegetables achieve a "meatier" flavor when they are roasted in the oven, and they don't take a long time as meat does. Steamed carrots are boring. Instead, try them roasted in honey-mustard sauce (page 153).

- Use flavorful ingredients where meat used to be. Raisins, currants and other dried fruits, imported black or stuffed green olives, capers and peperoncini, toasted nuts and seeds—all these can provide intense bursts of flavor.

- Don't forget the virtues of salt and freshly ground black pepper. Vegetarian food often gets blamed for being bland. The basics *are* bland—potatoes, rice, bulgur, pasta. Salt is necessary for flavor. A pepper grinder is also indispensable.

• Don't hesitate to grill or broil fruits and vegetables like asparagus, eggplant, potatoes, carrots, pineapple and peaches. Charcoal takes a long time to heat, but a gas or stove-top grill or an oven broiler cooks food faster than boiling or steaming and caramelizes the natural sugars in fresh produce, boosting taste. If you cook outdoors, you'll also get a hearty smoky taste.

• Use high temperatures. Higher heat cooks food faster. You might worry that things will burn more easily, but if you keep close watch over them, you can stir ingredients, remove them from the heat temporarily or turn the heat down if need be.

• Experiment with bold ethnic condiments. In the old days, supermarkets didn't carry anything much more interesting than tomato ketchup and pickle relish, but now they stock everything from Asian sesame oil and hoisin sauce to salsas, chutneys and herbed vinegars.

• Get a sharp knife for vegetarian and all other cooking. Better yet, get two, a big (chef's) knife and a small (paring) knife, and a cutting board to put underneath them. If you love cooking, you'll love it more using a sharp knife. If you hate cooking, sharp knives will get you in and out of the kitchen faster.

Salads

TWENTY YEARS AGO, if you were a vegetarian and joined a group of omnivores for dinner at a restaurant, you'd no doubt be relegated to the salad bar, there to choose among iceberg lettuce, cardboard tomatoes and greasy Thousand Island dressing.

Today, vegetarians eat as many salads as before, but they run the gamut from barley and mushrooms to grilled radicchio and fennel. In between is a wonderful array of tempting combinations that are healthy, speedy and flavorful.

Lettuce is ubiquitous, of course, so you can make salad all year. But don't forget that other seasons offer great vegetables that can also become salads. Time-stressed cooks in particular should consider the virtues of salads like sliced tomatoes or coleslaw for hectic weekday meals—these vegetables don't require elaborate washing and drying. Blanched green beans or broccoli lightly dressed with vinaigrette can sit for several days in the refrigerator—something lettuce can't do—ready at a moment's notice to become a substantial side dish.

Before they are marinated, though, tough vegetables may need blanching in boiling water. Blanching wakes up flavors and color and makes vegetables like green beans, broccoli, cauliflower, brussels sprouts and asparagus easier to chew. You'll need less dressing, which has two benefits: It saves you fat and calories and it allows the fresh taste of the vegetable to come through.

Grating hard vegetables or cutting them into fine slivers before marinating them also adds to the variety while making them more appealing. Kohlrabi, beets and carrots take little time to grate and require little cleanup. Kohlrabi benefits from a creamy dressing; beets like a vinaigrette with orange juice or rind, and carrots go well with ginger.

A LEAFY GREEN SALAD with a light dressing can be enhanced by just a few tidbits—red bell pepper and nuts or black olives and grated carrots. One of the best salads I ever ate was put together on a cool, rainy spring day from simple ingredients in the pantry. My host braved the chilly drizzle to pick mixed greens from his garden as his wife thinned her homemade pepper jelly for dressing and shaved Parmesan cheese over the top.

There are two keys to success with a lettuce salad: Choose interesting greens and dry them completely.

Use Bibb and red leaf lettuce more often than you do iceberg, and pick up some prewashed spinach or slivers of red cabbage from your supermarket salad bar. These ingredients are lightweight and won't cost you as much as store-bought potato salad or strawberries.

Wet leaves cause dressing to roll right to the bottom of the bowl. To dry them, use cloth towels, paper towels or, better yet, a salad spinner. The spinner can double as a storage container for refrigerated lettuce, so you might find it a worthwhile purchase.

Salad samplers make great vegetarian meals. Vary the selection by color, texture and type. A combination of corn and black bean salad, sliced tomatoes and marinated green beans is great at the height of summer. In the winter, consider a plate of marinated shredded beets, orange rounds and white bean salad.

Salads

Garlic Vinaigrette

VINAIGRETTE IS JUST A FANCY WORD FOR SALAD DRESSING. My basic vinaigrette is 3 parts olive oil and 1 part vinegar seasoned with salt and pepper. It's great not only for dressing lettuce but for other vegetables (hot and cold), for brushing on eggplant slabs before grilling or for seasoning pasta salads.

You can vary the formula, adding crumbled blue cheese or a smashed clove of garlic or both, if you like.

1 medium garlic clove
¼ cup olive oil
1 tablespoon vinegar
½ teaspoon salt
½ teaspoon freshly ground pepper, or to taste

Flatten garlic by pressing down on it firmly with the broad side of a knife. Place it in the bottom of a small jar and add remaining ingredients. Shake to dissolve salt.

Use immediately or store in the refrigerator.

Makes about ⅓ cup.

Balsamic and sherry vinegars are delicious, but any vinegar will work.

Honey-Mustard Vinaigrette

THIS POPULAR VINAIGRETTE has a nice, clingy consistency that coats lettuce leaves well. Serve as a dressing for leafy salad, for hot or cold vegetables or for fruit salads.

- ½ cup olive oil or vegetable oil
- 2 tablespoons vinegar (any kind)
- 2 tablespoons honey
- 1 tablespoon Dijon-style mustard
- Salt and freshly ground pepper to taste

Combine all ingredients in a small jar and shake to dissolve honey and distribute mustard. Use immediately or store in the refrigerator.

Makes ¾ cup.

You can substitute any spicy European-style mustard for the Dijon.

Greens with Honey-Soy Dressing

THIS GREEN SALAD is an Asian twist on the standard tossed version. With a dressing of soy sauce, honey and ginger, it makes a good complement to main dishes that have an Asian flavor to them, like fried rice or lo mein, or even a simple baked potato. This is a light salad. To make it richer, add Spicy Nuts (page 29) or toasted sunflower seeds.

8 cups salad greens, washed and dried
1 bunch green onions, trimmed and minced
½ cup chopped red bell pepper (½ large pepper)

A salad spinner makes quick work of drying salad greens.

Dressing

3 tablespoons olive oil or vegetable oil
1 tablespoon soy sauce
1 tablespoon honey
Juice of 1 lemon
1-3 teaspoons peeled, minced fresh ginger

Place salad greens, green onions and pepper in a salad bowl or on individual plates.

To make dressing: In a small jar, combine oil, soy sauce, honey, lemon juice and ginger. Shake well to combine and dissolve honey. Pour over salad greens and serve.

Serves 4 to 6.

Green Salad with Pears and Blue Cheese

MY FAVORITE GREEN SALAD of all is made with leafy greens, slices of pear, crumbles of blue cheese or feta cheese and perhaps a scattering of pine nuts or toasted pecans.

- 3 tablespoons chopped pecans, pine nuts or other nuts (or substitute Spicy Nuts, page 29)
- ¼ cup olive oil, vegetable oil or fancy nut oil
- 1 tablespoon vinegar (any kind—red wine vinegar or balsamic vinegar are good)
- ½ teaspoon salt
- ¼ teaspoon freshly ground pepper
- 8 cups salad greens (torn leafy green lettuce, such as romaine or Bibb), washed and dried
- 1 ripe pear (any kind)
- ¼ cup crumbled blue cheese or feta cheese

Prepare the greens by washing, wrapping in toweling and refrigerating in a plastic bag or in a salad spinner.

If using plain nuts, toast in a 350-degree oven for 10 minutes, or until they smell fragrant, or stir them in a dry skillet over medium-high heat on top of the stove for 3 to 4 minutes. Set aside.

Combine oil, vinegar, salt and pepper in a small jar. Screw the lid on tightly, shake to dissolve dressing and set aside.

Divide lettuce among 4 salad plates (or put in a salad bowl). Quarter the pear, remove the fibrous core and seeds (peel, if desired), and slice each quarter in thirds or fourths. Arrange pears in a pinwheel on lettuce. Sprinkle with cheese and toasted nuts, drizzle with dressing and serve.

Serves 4.

Pizza Salad

PIZZA SALAD GETS ITS NAME FROM ITS FLEXIBLE NATURE. Like the pizza we order over the phone, this dish can get different toppings to reflect your mood. When my family buys pizza, we like mushrooms, green pepper and olives. If that sounds salty to you—especially with the added cheese—leave off the olives. Or you can even add "the works."

- **2 tablespoons olive oil**
- **2 teaspoons vinegar (any kind)**
- **¼ teaspoon salt**
- **¼ teaspoon freshly ground pepper**
- **1 tablespoon chopped olives or peperoncini pickles**
- **6 cups salad greens (romaine, spinach, leaf lettuce)**
- **¼ cup sliced mushrooms**
- **¼ cup chopped green bell pepper**
- **¼-½ cup shredded provolone or mozzarella cheese**

> **Peperoncini are pickled peppers and can be found bottled near the other pickles and olives in your supermarket.**

Combine oil, vinegar, salt, pepper and olives or peperoncini in a small jar or bowl and shake or stir to dissolve salt.

Put greens in a salad bowl or on individual salad plates. Add mushrooms and green pepper and toss with dressing. Sprinkle with cheese and serve.

Serves 4.

Greek Peasant Salad

GREEK PEASANT SALAD is a cinch to make when summer vegetables are at their height. It's just cut-up tomatoes and cucumbers with feta cheese and olives added for richness and flavor.

Dressing

- 3 tablespoons olive oil or vegetable oil
- 1 tablespoon vinegar (red wine vinegar is good)
- ¼ teaspoon salt
- ¼ teaspoon freshly ground pepper
- 1 teaspoon dried oregano

Salad

- 1 cucumber, peeled, if desired, and cut into chunks
- 1 pint cherry tomatoes, halved
- About ¼ cup crumbled feta cheese
- ¼ cup chopped pitted imported black olives or stuffed green olives

> • • •
>
> Leftovers can be stuffed into pita pockets or combined with cold noodles to make pasta salad.
>
> • • •

To make dressing: Combine dressing ingredients in a small jar and shake until salt is dissolved. Set aside.

To make salad: You may want to seed cucumber by cutting it in half lengthwise and scooping out seeds with a small spoon or blunt knife. Combine all ingredients in a bowl and toss to mix. Drizzle with dressing.

Serves 6. ~ Serve as part of a vegetable plate or on a bed of shredded salad greens as a starter. Or accompany it with steamed artichokes and rice or with noodles seasoned with lemon and herbs.

Nutty Rice Salad

I COME FROM MINT JULEP COUNTRY, where mint in the garden can take over a plot if you don't watch it. From late spring until the sun's rays get short again, we have all the mint we want, and this salad is a good way to use it. It has a nutty sweetness with overtones of green onion, and it's good with sandwiches, on a vegetable plate or as part of a salad sampler. If you don't have fresh mint, use a little dried.

- **¾ cup wild-rice mix**
- **2¼ cups water or vegetable broth**
- **½ cup chopped pecans**
- **⅓ cup orange juice**
- **2 tablespoons vegetable oil**
- **1 cup dried currants**
- **1 bunch green onions, trimmed and minced (about ½ cup)**
- **¼ cup fresh mint or 1 tablespoon dried**

> **Long-grain and wild-rice mix comes in 6-ounce packages with an herb seasoning. Just use the rice (not the seasoning) in this recipe.**

Combine rice and water or broth in a small saucepan and bring to a boil. Reduce the heat to low, cover and cook for 25 minutes, or until rice is tender. If there's any liquid left in the pan, drain rice in a wire strainer.

Meanwhile, toast pecans in a 350-degree oven for 10 minutes, or until they smell toasty, or stir them constantly in a dry skillet over medium-high heat on top of the stove for 3 to 4 minutes.

Transfer to a bowl and mix with remaining ingredients. Serve cold or at room temperature.

Serves 8.

Marinated Green Beans

THIS SALAD CAN BE MADE a day or two ahead and refrigerated until you need it. In fact, you can double the recipe if you want and keep it in the fridge to have handy when you need something green—to serve as a side for dinner, for lunch or for a healthful snack. It's my salad of choice when beans are relentlessly prolific in the garden, but it's good made with frozen green beans too. You can substitute broccoli for beans.

1 tablespoon sesame seeds (optional)
1 pound fresh green beans, cut into 2-inch lengths, or 1 pound frozen
¼ cup olive oil or vegetable oil
1½ tablespoons vinegar (any kind)
½ teaspoon salt, or to taste
¼ teaspoon freshly ground pepper
½ cup chopped red onion, or to taste

• • •

You can make this with leftover cooked green beans. Toasted sesame or sunflower seeds are good in it.

• • •

Toast sesame seeds, if using, in a 350-degree oven until light brown, about 15 minutes, or stir them constantly in a dry skillet over medium-high heat on top of the stove for 3 to 4 minutes.

Cook beans for about 8 minutes in boiling water, or until they are tender but still firm (total cooking time depends on the size and type of bean—thin, young beans take 5 minutes or less; large pole beans take longer). Drain, rinse with cool water and drain well. (If you're using frozen beans, follow package directions for cooking them.)

Meanwhile, combine oil, vinegar, salt and pepper in a small jar or bowl and shake or stir to dissolve salt.

Toss beans in a bowl with dressing. Serve topped with red onion and sesame seeds, if desired. Serve warm, at room temperature or chilled.

Serves 4 to 6.

Tabbouleh

TABBOULEH WAS PROBABLY the first ethnic dish I ever ate in a restaurant. It's a wonderfully refreshing dish. The fresh parsley is a must, but the mint is optional. If you like mint and have it in your yard or can get some at the supermarket, you can add more to this dish.

2 cups water
1 teaspoon salt, plus more to taste
1½ cups bulgur
1 bunch green onions, trimmed
1 cup chopped fresh parsley
¼ cup chopped fresh mint or 1 tablespoon dried (optional)
2 ripe tomatoes
Juice of 2 lemons
2-3 tablespoons olive oil
Freshly ground pepper to taste

Make this dish more substantial by adding chopped canned chick-peas.

Bring water to boil with 1 teaspoon salt. Add bulgur, cover, remove from heat and set aside for 5 minutes or more, until bulgur is chewy but tender.

Chop green onions, parsley and mint, if using, and put them in a medium-size bowl. Core tomatoes, cut in half and, holding cut side down, squeeze gently to remove excess seeds (don't worry about getting them all out). Chop tomatoes fine and add them to the bowl along with lemon juice and oil. Add bulgur; toss to combine. Season with salt and pepper. Serve at room temperature or chilled; this salad improves as it sits. It will keep for up to 1 week.

Serves 4 to 6. ~ Serve as a side dish alongside smooth, creamy soups or with summer vegetables, such as Quick Fried Squash (page 162).

Potato Salad with Dill, Sour Cream and Capers

PEELING POTATOES SLOWS A RECIPE DOWN, so I try to skip the step if I can. In general, I peel Idaho baking potatoes if their skins seem very thick, but I rarely peel red-skinned or yellow-flesh potatoes.

Red wine vinegar is a good choice for this potato salad, but any type will work. You can also mix the sour cream with mayonnaise or plain low-fat yogurt, or thin it with a little buttermilk.

- 2 pounds potatoes
- 1 tablespoon vinegar (any kind)
- 1 shallot or 3-4 green onions, minced
- 2 tablespoons fresh dill or 2 teaspoons dried
- 2-3 tablespoons capers
- ½ cup sour cream, or to taste (nonfat can be used)

> The best potatoes for this are red-skinned or yellow Finn, but any potato will work.

Boil potatoes with skins on, until done (they should yield easily when you insert a paring knife). When potatoes are cool enough to handle, peel them, if desired, and cut them into slices or chunks.

Sprinkle with vinegar, shallot or green onions, dill, capers and a little of the caper juice. Stir in sour cream. Serve at room temperature or chilled.

Serves 6 to 8.

Honey-Mustard Carrot Salad

WALNUTS MAKE THIS SALAD of grated carrots savory and rich, while a touch of honey brings out its sweetness.

- **¼ cup chopped walnuts**
- **2 tablespoons apple cider vinegar (or any kind)**
- **1 tablespoon Dijon-style mustard**
- **½ teaspoon sugar or honey**
- **¼ teaspoon salt**
- **1 garlic clove, minced**
- **2 tablespoons vegetable oil**
- **1 pound carrots**

Toast walnuts in a 350-degree oven for 10 minutes, or until they smell fragrant, or stir constantly in a dry skillet over medium-high heat on top of the stove for 3 to 4 minutes. Cool.

Combine vinegar, mustard, sugar or honey, salt and garlic in a blender or small jar with a tight-fitting lid.

Turn on the blender and slowly add oil or pour oil in the jar and shake—the dressing will be opaque but not thick like mayonnaise. If you shake the dressing, it won't be as creamy-looking but will still taste good.

Peel carrots and grate them on the large side of the grater. Toss with dressing and top with toasted nuts.

Serves 4 ~ Serve as a side salad to any dish that doesn't have carrots or nuts, such as Speedy Baked Potatoes (page 76) or Greek Pita Pizza (page 174).

Sweet-and-Sour Cucumber Salad

THESE SWEET-AND-SOUR CUCUMBERS are a fresher version of the bread-and-butter pickles that are likely to accompany many rural Southern vegetable plates. Like pickles, they don't traditionally have oil added to them, but you can stir some in for flavor, if you want.

- 2 medium cucumbers
- ½-1 medium yellow onion
- 2 tablespoons vinegar (any kind)
- 2 tablespoons sugar
- ½ teaspoon salt
- ¼ teaspoon freshly ground pepper
- 1-2 tablespoons olive oil or vegetable oil (optional)

> Discarding the cucumber seeds will cut down on the juice.

Peel cucumbers, if desired, slice them in half lengthwise and use a small spoon to scrape the seeds out. Discard seeds, then slice cucumbers about ¼ inch thick. Slice onion ⅛ inch thick and break rings apart.

In a medium bowl, combine vinegar, sugar, salt and pepper. Stir to dissolve sugar, then add cucumbers and onions. Add oil, if desired. Serve at room temperature or cold. This salad keeps well in the refrigerator for several days.

Serves 6. ~ Serve as part of a salad plate or vegetable plate, or as a side salad to hot potatoes, rice or pasta dishes. Or add a dash of yogurt or sour cream and serve with curries.

Savory Broccoli Salad

THERE ARE VARIOUS RENDITIONS of sturdy broccoli salads circulating among family cooks. Most of them have lots of mayonnaise and sugar, and many are made with uncooked broccoli.

I'll tell you a secret that will help you reduce the fat: blanch the vegetables. The salad will also taste better if these tough vegetables are cooked a little first.

Salt
1 medium head broccoli (about 1½ pounds)
½ cup mayonnaise
1 tablespoon vinegar (any kind; apple cider vinegar is good)
½ cup raisins
½ cup toasted, salted sunflower seeds
½ red onion, thinly sliced

> **You can substitute green beans or cauliflower for the broccoli.**

Fill a 3-quart saucepan with about 3 inches water. Salt water and bring to a boil.

Meanwhile, cut broccoli head into florets. Peel stems, if using, and cut them into small chunks. (A salad made of florets is prettier and perhaps more aesthetically appealing, but you may not want to throw out stems: Once peeled, they make good eating.) You should have about 3 cups.

When water boils, add broccoli. Cover the pan for 1 minute, then remove the cover and cook broccoli for 4 to 5 minutes more, depending on how big florets are; broccoli should be tender and bright green. Drain well.

As broccoli cooks, put mayonnaise and vinegar in a large bowl. Stir. Add drained broccoli and raisins. Add ¼ cup sunflower seeds and toss briefly. Top with red onion and sprinkle remaining ¼ cup sunflower seeds over broccoli before serving.

Serves 4. ~ Serve with baked potatoes.

Spicy Nuts

A FEW OF THESE SPICY NUTS go a long way in a tossed salad and make a great addition to steamed vegetables. Don't leave them long on the counter after you make them—anyone who spots them can't resist taking a handful.

The sugar coating burns easily if the fire is too high under the pan. The coating should be deep brown, not black.

- **⅔ cup pecans (or substitute sunflower seeds, walnuts, almonds)**
- **2 teaspoons vegetable oil**
- **1 tablespoon sugar**
- **½ teaspoon freshly ground pepper**
- **⅛ teaspoon cayenne**
- **2 teaspoons soy sauce**

> If you double this recipe, use only 3 teaspoons oil. Store extra nuts in a jar or a plastic container in the freezer.

Toast nuts in a 400-degree oven for 10 minutes, or until they smell fragrant. Chop coarsely if using pecans or walnut halves (smaller nuts don't need chopping).

Combine oil, sugar, black pepper, cayenne and soy sauce in a small pan. Stir over medium-low heat to dissolve sugar, then bring to a boil (this takes just a minute or so). Boil for 1 minute, then add nuts, stirring to coat. Reduce the heat to low and cook for 2 to 3 minutes, until liquid has evaporated and nuts are coated. Cool nuts before sprinkling over salads or cooked vegetables.

Makes ⅔ cup.

Soups

Soup is a great place to start convincing yourself and others that vegetarian food is not only flavorful and easy but inexpensive, satisfying and nutritious. For cooks who wilt at the thought of making several dishes in the few hectic moments they have to cook dinner, these selections make easy dinners.

Soup will likely reduce your shopping requirements. It can generally be made with what you have in the house. With an onion, olive oil, a few fresh or frozen vegetables, a can of tomatoes and perhaps some beans, you're well on your way to a fabulous meal.

Good soups are easy to prepare. Decent broths can be purchased at the store; adding fresh onion and garlic gives them a boost. You needn't be skillful with a knife because the soup doesn't care if one carrot chunk is a little bigger than another. Precise timing and precise measuring are unnecessary.

Soups democratically accept foods that your family might not eat otherwise. I've sneaked diced turnips into vegetable soup and whole-grain bulgur into chili, and my children have been healthier but no wiser.

Cleanup is also a cinch. You rely only on your sharp knife and a pot for a soup. If you use your blender, whir water in it when you're finished to make washing easier.

Soups generally reheat well, so you can refrigerate leftovers for a day or two, carrying them to lunch for warming in a microwave or serving them for dinner another night.

Top your soups with a flourish. Yogurt or sour cream add creamy coolness to a hot and spicy soup. To heighten the appeal, garnish with minced red bell pepper or red onion or chopped fresh cilantro or chives. Grated cheese and/or toasted sunflower seeds lend richness to broth- or water-based soups.

Floating croutons or crushed tortilla chips on top is the grown-up version of breaking saltines into cream of tomato soup. Fat-free tortilla chips come in a variety of flavors, so you can spice up your soups without adding fat.

Soups

Creamy Tomato Soup

THIS TOMATO SOUP is a great dish to serve to a mixed group. Vegans, who avoid all animal products, will appreciate it because it doesn't contain any, yet it won't seem outlandish to prime-rib fans.

3 tablespoons vegetable oil or olive oil
2 medium onions, peeled and sliced
3 medium potatoes, scrubbed and cubed
2½ cups water
1 28-ounce can tomatoes
2 teaspoons sugar
1 teaspoon salt
⅛ teaspoon ground cloves
Freshly ground pepper to taste
Sour cream or plain yogurt (optional)

> Acidic foods, such as tomatoes, will slow the cooking of starch in potatoes, so add the tomatoes last.

Heat oil in a large saucepan over medium heat and add onions. Cook over high heat, until they are translucent, about 5 minutes, stirring occasionally. Add potatoes (you should have about 3 cups) and 2 cups of water. Cover, bring to a boil, then reduce the heat to low and simmer for 20 minutes, or until potatoes are tender.

Put potato mixture in a blender, add remaining ½ cup water and blend until smooth, about 15 seconds. Remove the top from the blender, stir briefly, return the top and blend. Repeat until mixture is creamy, blending once or twice more. Return mixture to the saucepan.

Add tomatoes to the blender with sugar, salt, cloves and pepper. Blend until smooth, about 30 seconds. Add to the saucepan and heat through. Serve topped with sour cream or yogurt, if desired.

Serves 4 to 6. ~ Serve with My Hero (page 186) or another vegetable sandwich.

Better-Than-Canned Tomato Soup

WHEN YOU NEED SOMETHING QUICK, warm and delicious, this is the ticket. It's much less elaborate than the previous version. The small amount of fennel seed in this soup gives it a rich flavor but isn't overpowering.

- 2 tablespoons olive oil
- 2 garlic cloves
- ½ teaspoon fennel seeds
- 1 28-ounce can tomatoes (or 2 pounds fresh tomatoes, peeled and cored)
- Salt and freshly ground pepper to taste

Heat oil in a medium pot. Mince garlic and add it to the pot with fennel seeds and cook over medium heat until garlic is aromatic, about 3 minutes.

Add tomatoes, stir, then pour into a blender. Blend for 30 seconds.

Return to the pot and heat through. Season with salt and pepper as needed.

Serves 2. ~ Serve with cheese sandwiches or green salad and toast.

> This really needs fresh garlic; don't substitute powder or flakes.

Creamy Chick-Pea Soup with Garlic and Lemon

Mother Nature had lemons and garlic in mind when she created chick-peas. This soup makes dinner a cinch.

- 4 large garlic cloves, minced
- 2 tablespoons olive oil or vegetable oil
- 2 15-to-19-ounce cans chick-peas (also called garbanzo beans)
- Juice of 1 lemon
- 1 teaspoon dried oregano
- 1 teaspoon salt
- ¼ teaspoon crushed red pepper (or substitute cayenne or Tabasco sauce)
- About 1 cup water
- 2-3 tablespoons chutney
- Toasted sesame seeds (see page 23) or crumbled feta cheese (optional)

> Leftovers from this soup are good with a little curry powder stirred in. You'll need to thin it with broth or water.

In a large saucepan over medium-high heat, cook garlic in oil until golden, 3 to 5 minutes.

Add chick-peas with their liquid and heat through. Add lemon juice, oregano, salt and red pepper. Simmer for 10 minutes. Put mixture in a blender and blend until smooth. Return to the pan, stir in water and heat through. Add more water to thin to desired consistency (I like it thick).

Serve in warm bowls, stirring in a little chutney and sprinkling with toasted sesame seeds or feta cheese, if desired.

Serves 4.

"Cream" of Sesame Spinach Soup

•••••••••••••••••

THIS SOUP IS CREAMY BUT CREAMLESS. It's thick and dark green with a background flavor of sesame seeds. Sesame seeds are inexpensive when you buy them in bulk at a health food store, but if you do so, be sure to store them in the freezer. They'll keep longer.

A blender is the best tool for making this soup and many other purees. If you don't have one, use a food processor or a hand mixer to break up the lumpiest lumps and call it "chunky spinach soup."

¼ cup sesame seeds
2 tablespoons vegetable oil
1 medium onion
2 medium potatoes, unpeeled
1 10-ounce package frozen chopped spinach
3 cups water
Salt and freshly ground pepper to taste
⅛ teaspoon grated nutmeg

> • • •
>
> **You can substitute asparagus for spinach.**
>
> • • •

Combine seeds and oil in a large saucepan and cook over medium heat as you chop onion. When sesame seeds are light brown (about 5 minutes), add onions.

Meanwhile, cube potatoes in about 1-inch pieces. Add to the pan and cook for about 5 minutes, stirring occasionally, or until onion is translucent and potatoes begin to stick to the bottom of the pan.

Add spinach, 2 cups water, salt, pepper and nutmeg. Cover and cook for 2 minutes, then turn the heat to low and simmer for 20 minutes. Potatoes should be tender. If not, cook until they are.

Pour mixture into a blender and blend for 30 seconds. Stir, then blend for another 30 seconds. Pour mixture back into the pan, add remaining 1 cup water and heat through. Season with nutmeg and more salt and pepper.

Serves 4. ~ Serve with Biscuits (page 200) or rolls, with fresh strawberries for dessert.

Italian Vegetable Soup

THIS SOUP GETS AN INSTANT ITALIAN FLAVOR when you use prepared spaghetti sauce, but it'll taste great with plain tomato sauce too. Substitute 10 ounces of frozen peas and carrots for the fresh zucchini and carrot, if you like.

- 2 tablespoons olive oil or vegetable oil
- 1 small green bell pepper, cored and diced (about ¼-inch pieces)
- 1 zucchini (about 7 inches long), cubed (about ¼-inch pieces)
- 1 carrot, peeled and diced small
- 1 15-to-19-ounce can chick-peas (also called garbanzo beans)
- 1 14½-ounce can peeled diced tomatoes
- 1 cup prepared spaghetti sauce or canned tomato sauce
- 1 teaspoon dried thyme leaves
- 2 14-to-16-ounce cans vegetable broth
- 3 cups water
- 1 cup rotini (corkscrew noodles)
- Salt and freshly ground pepper to taste
- Grated Parmesan cheese (optional)

Heat oil in a large pot. Add green pepper, zucchini and carrot and stir. Add chick-peas with their liquid, tomatoes, spaghetti or tomato sauce, thyme, vegetable broth and water. Bring to a boil.

Add noodles and simmer for 20 minutes, or until tender. Season with salt and pepper. Serve topped with a little grated Parmesan cheese, if desired.

Serves 6 to 8. ~ Serve with Garlic (Cheese) Bread (page 196).

Sweet Potato Soup

BLENDING SWEET POTATOES turns them silky smooth. The jalapeño pepper adds a spicy bite at the end, but if you're a heat-o-phobe, you can forgo it.

- 2 14-to-16-ounce cans vegetable broth
- 2 pounds sweet potatoes
- 2 red or yellow bell peppers
- 1 small jalapeño pepper
- 2 large garlic cloves, minced
- ½ teaspoon dried thyme leaves
- Water or buttermilk (optional)
- Salt and freshly ground pepper to taste
- Sour cream (optional)

> • • •
>
> Do not substitute green peppers for red or yellow, as they will turn the soup a strange color.
>
> • • •

Put broth in a large saucepan and bring to a boil. Meanwhile, slice sweet potatoes ½ inch thick (don't bother peeling them, but trim any hard spots or root fibers) and add to the pot. Return to a boil, cover and simmer until tender, about 15 minutes.

Meanwhile, stem, seed and chop bell peppers and jalapeño. Chop them coarsely; they'll be blended later. Add them to sweet potatoes as you prepare them. Add garlic and thyme and stir.

When sweet potatoes are tender, place mixture in a blender or food processor and blend until smooth (if using a blender, do this in batches). Thin with water or buttermilk, if desired, to the consistency you prefer. Season with salt and pepper. Top with a dollop of sour cream, if you like.

Serves 4 to 6 as a main dish. ~ **Serve warm with Simple Corn Bread (page 198).**

Tortilla Soup

Cumin and canned green chilies provide a Mexican twist to this vegetable soup. Tortilla chips add crunch and substance. If you have fresh corn, of course you should use that, but frozen works admirably as well. This is also good topped with a little grated Monterey Jack or Cheddar cheese.

- 3 tablespoons olive oil or vegetable oil
- 1 yellow onion, chopped
- 1 green or red bell pepper, cored and chopped
- 3 large garlic cloves, chopped
- 4 teaspoons ground cumin
- 2 teaspoons freshly ground pepper
- 6 cups canned vegetable broth or water
- 1 28-ounce can crushed tomatoes
- 3 4-ounce cans chopped mild green chilies
- 2 cups frozen corn
- Tortilla chips

> Adding baked, salted tortilla chips to this soup keeps the fat low but the flavor high. Experiment with different flavors.

Heat oil in a large saucepan on high heat. Add onion, green or red pepper, garlic, cumin and black pepper. Cook, stirring often, about 5 minutes. Vegetables should be soft.

Add broth or water, tomatoes and green chilies. Cook for 15 minutes more to let flavors blend. Add corn and cook for 5 minutes. Top with tortilla chips and serve.

Serves 4 to 6. ~ Serve with Cheesy Quesadillas (page 185).

Vegetable-Rice Soup

WHEN THE WEATHER CALLS for a pot of vegetable soup, this is an ideal candidate. Add a chunked zucchini or a diced potato, if desired.

- ½ cup lentils
- 7 cups water
- 2 teaspoons salt
- 1 cup brown rice (or substitute white rice)
- 2 medium onions, chopped
- 2 carrots, peeled and chopped
- 1 green bell pepper, seeded and chopped
- 4-6 large garlic cloves, minced
- 1 teaspoon dried basil
- 1 teaspoon dried thyme leaves
- 1 28-ounce can crushed tomatoes

> This soup is good served with a dash of vinegar or a spoonful of sour cream.

Rinse lentils in a colander under running water. Add to a large pot with water and salt and bring to a boil over high heat. If you're using brown rice, add it now.

Add onions, carrots, pepper, garlic, basil and thyme. Bring to a boil, reduce the heat to low and simmer, uncovered, for 20 minutes.

If you're using white rice, add it now, along with the tomatoes, and cook for 20 minutes more, or until rice and lentils are tender. Serve hot. This freezes well.

Serves 6. ~ Serve with Simple Corn Bread (page 198) or Biscuits (page 200) or with grilled-cheese-and-tomato sandwiches.

Split Pea-Barley Soup

SPLIT PEAS AND BARLEY are an ancient combination, but the addition of soy sauce makes this soup a little out of the ordinary. Soy sauce is useful in vegetarian cooking because the fermented soybeans lend a "meaty" dimension to food that salt can't give.

Barley is a whole grain that's chewy, nutty and silky at the same time. The barley sold in the supermarket is usually medium or fine pearled. "Medium" and "fine" refer to the size, and the size of the grain will affect cooking times, although not a tremendous amount. Pearled barley has been processed to make it cook more quickly than ordinary. Quick-cooking barley is faster yet, ready in 10 or 15 minutes.

If you don't have a lemon reamer, juice lemons by holding a half upside down in your hands with your thumbs on the end and your fingers on the cut side. Squeeze up with your fingers. The juice should flow through your fingers, but the seeds get caught.

- 3 tablespoons olive oil
- 1 medium onion, chopped
- 2 carrots, chopped
- 1½ cups split peas, rinsed
- ½ cup regular or quick-cooking barley
- 8 cups water
- Grated zest and juice of 1 lemon
- 2 tablespoons soy sauce
- 2 teaspoons dried thyme leaves
- 1 teaspoon salt
- ½ teaspoon freshly ground pepper

• • •

If you don't have split peas, substitute lentils.

• • •

Heat oil over high heat in a large saucepan. Add onion and carrots and cook, stirring occasionally, for 5 minutes, until softened. Add split peas, barley (if using quick-cooking barley, add it later) and water. Bring to a boil.

Add lemon zest to the pan along with soy sauce, thyme, salt and pepper. Bring to a boil, reduce the heat and simmer for 40 minutes, or until split peas and barley are tender. If using quick-cooking barley, add it during the last 10 to 15 minutes of cooking. Remove from the heat and stir in lemon juice. This freezes well.

Serves 6 to 8. ~ Serve with open-faced toasted cheese sandwiches on English muffin halves.

Blender Broccoli Soup

LITTLE BITS OF BROCCOLI make this soup slightly chewy. It's delicious served with a little sour cream (even low-fat sour cream) on top.

- **1** **10-ounce package frozen chopped broccoli, thawed**
- **3** **tablespoons all-purpose flour**
- **½** **teaspoon dried basil**
- **½** **teaspoon salt**
- **½** **teaspoon freshly ground pepper**
- **1½** **cups milk**
- **½** **cup water**
- **½** **cup grated Swiss or Cheddar cheese**

> **The recipe may be doubled, but mix each batch separately in the blender.**

Combine broccoli, flour, basil, salt, pepper and 1 cup of milk in a blender. Blend well for at least 30 seconds. Pour into a saucepan with remaining ½ cup milk (do not clean the blender) and cook over medium-high heat, stirring often, until mixture begins to boil.

Add water to the blender and whir for a few seconds to rinse it out. Add to soup. Once mixture boils, turn heat to low and let simmer gently for 2 minutes. Remove from the heat, stir in cheese and pour into serving bowls.

Serves 2 to 4. ~ Serve with Savory Chick-Pea Pita Pockets (page 188).

Curried Corn Chowder

Curry complements corn chowder because both the onion and the corn are sweet. For the right balance, don't be shy with the cayenne. You can use fresh corn, if you have it, or substitute plain canned or frozen.

- **2 tablespoons olive oil or vegetable oil**
- **1 large onion, finely chopped**
- **1 teaspoon curry powder**
- **4 medium potatoes, peeled and diced in ½-inch cubes**
- **1 celery rib, finely chopped**
- **2 14-to-16-ounce cans vegetable broth or 3-4 cups water**
- **1 teaspoon salt**
- **½ teaspoon freshly ground pepper**
- **¼ teaspoon cayenne**
- **1 15-ounce can cream-style corn**
- **2 cups milk (skim is fine)**
- **Hot pepper sauce (optional)**

Try this soup with 1 to 2 teaspoons chutney stirred in.

Heat oil in a large pot over high heat. Add onion and curry powder and cook, stirring frequently, until onion is translucent, about 5 minutes.

Add potatoes and celery. Add vegetable broth or water, salt, pepper and cayenne and simmer over medium heat until potatoes are tender, about 15 to 20 minutes. Add corn and milk and heat through.

Ladle into hot soup bowls and pass hot pepper sauce at the table, if desired.

Serves 4. ~ Serve with raw vegetables and toasted pita triangles.

Vegetable-Bean Soup with Black Olives

I THINK OF THIS as a winter soup because of the beans and cabbage, but it could be made suitable for summer by adding eggplant and potato chunks. If you stick with the cabbage, be advised that it cooks up very sweet, so you'll need every bit of salt the recipe calls for.

- 3 tablespoons olive oil or vegetable oil
- 1 cup shredded cabbage
- 1 small green bell pepper, chopped
- 3 large garlic cloves, minced
- 1½ teaspoons salt
- 1½ teaspoons dried basil
- 1 teaspoon dried thyme leaves
- Freshly ground pepper to taste
- About 4 cups water
- 1 16-ounce can Great Northern beans
- ¼ cup (½ of a 6-ounce can) tomato paste
- ½ cup imported black olives or stuffed green olives

> Freeze leftover tomato paste. Use it later in Curried Chick-Peas and Potatoes (page 82) or in Aromatic Persian Rice (page 56).

Heat oil in a large pot or Dutch oven. Add cabbage, green pepper and garlic. Sprinkle with salt, basil, thyme and pepper, and cook for 15 minutes over medium-high heat. The vegetables should shrink and soften.

Add remaining ingredients, except olives, and heat through. Add more water if the soup is too thick for your taste.

Pit and slice olives as soup heats. Stir them in at the last minute or sprinkle them over the top.

Serves 4 to 6. ~ Serve with Garlic (Cheese) Bread (page 196).

Chick-Pea and Zucchini Soup

HAVING GROWN UP ON VEGETABLE SOUPS made with meat broths, I was ready to be disappointed by soups made without it. That's narrow thinking indeed! Even when you don't spend a lot of time simmering vegetable broths, you can create satisfying soups.

- **2 tablespoons olive oil or vegetable oil**
- **1 medium red onion, diced small**
- **3 garlic cloves, minced**
- **1 teaspoon dried thyme leaves**
- **1 16-ounce can tomatoes**
- **1 16-ounce can chick-peas (also called garbanzo beans)**
- **1 teaspoon chili powder**
- **Salt and freshly ground pepper to taste**
- **8 cups water or other liquid (including liquid from tomatoes)**
- **3 zucchini (no longer than 7 inches)**
- **2 ounces spaghetti, broken into 2-inch lengths (about ¾ cup)**

> • • •
>
> **Substitute a regular onion if you don't have a red one.**
>
> • • •

Heat oil in a large pot. Add onion, garlic and thyme and cook over high heat until onion is soft, about 3 minutes. Drain tomatoes (saving liquid) and dice them small. Add to the pot along with chick-peas, chili powder, salt, pepper and 8 cups liquid.

Prepare zucchini by cutting it into 3-by-¼-inch matchsticks. Add to the pot, then add spaghetti.

Bring to a boil, reduce the heat to medium and cook until spaghetti is tender, about 15 minutes. Serve hot.

Serves 4. ~ Serve with whole-wheat rolls.

Good Luck Soup

SOUTHERNERS EAT BLACK-EYED PEAS for good luck—consuming them is supposed to make you rich. Everyone else should like this soup because it tastes great, quickly dispelling the traditional idea that you have to add ham to beans to make them taste good.

2 tablespoons olive oil or vegetable oil
1 medium onion, chopped
2 16-ounce cans black-eyed peas
1 red bell pepper, cored and chopped
4 large garlic cloves, minced
2 teaspoons dried basil
1 teaspoon salt
1 teaspoon dried thyme leaves
½ teaspoon freshly ground pepper
½ teaspoon crushed red pepper
7 cups water

You can substitute green pepper for the red bell pepper.

Heat oil in a large pot over high heat. Add onion and cook, stirring frequently, until they begin to brown. Add remaining ingredients.

Bring to a boil, reduce the heat to low and simmer, uncovered, for about 15 minutes, or until soup is heated through.

Serves 4. ~ Serve with rolls or Cheesy Quesadillas (page 185), omitting the pimiento. It's also good with Tabbouleh (page 24).

Greek White Bean Soup

In Greece, families abstain from meat every Friday as well as on many holidays and saints' days. I got this recipe from a Greek woman who prepares it every Friday night for dinner. I was suspicious at first; the ingredients didn't seem promising. But the whole is greater than the sum of its parts—as is so often true in ethnic recipes that have survived for centuries. It is not only delicious, but it also requires very little effort.

- ¼ cup olive oil
- 1 celery rib
- 1 carrot
- 1 onion
- About ½ cup chopped fresh parsley
- 2 16-ounce cans Great Northern beans
- 4 cups water
- 1 6-ounce can tomato paste (about ½ cup)
- ¼ teaspoon crushed red pepper or ground red pepper
- Salt and freshly ground pepper to taste

Heat oil in a large pot over medium-high heat. Chop celery, carrot and onion, adding them to the pot as you prepare them. Stir after each addition and cook, stirring occasionally, until vegetables are softened, about 10 minutes.

Add parsley, beans, water, tomato paste, red pepper, salt and lots of black pepper. Bring to a boil, reduce the heat and simmer for 15 to 30 minutes (the longer the time, the more the flavors will meld).

Serves 6. ~ Serve with rolls, Cheese-Mustard Muffins (page 197) or Breadsticks (page 194).

Quick Chili

Bulgur is made of whole wheatberries that have been cracked, cooked and dried so they reconstitute quickly. In this dish, it takes the role of ground beef.

- 1 cup tomato juice
- ½ cup bulgur
- 2 tablespoons olive oil
- 3-5 garlic cloves, minced
- 1 teaspoon ground cumin
- 1 teaspoon dried oregano
- 1 16-ounce can red beans in chili sauce
- 1 4-ounce can chopped mild green chilies
- 1 16-ounce can tomatoes

In the South and Midwest, chili is often served with spaghetti. You can serve this dish with noodles, if you like.

Bring tomato juice to a boil in a medium saucepan (you can do this in a bowl in the microwave, about 1½ minutes on high). Remove from heat and add bulgur.

Heat oil in another medium saucepan over medium-high heat. Add garlic and cook until it becomes golden, about 2 minutes. Add cumin and oregano and cook, stirring, for about 30 seconds. Add beans, chilies and bulgur and stir to mix. Add tomatoes, squeezing them through your fingers or chopping them fine as you add them. Add all their juice and cook for 15 to 30 minutes, adding water to thin to the desired consistency.

Serves 4.

To make burritos with leftover chili: Use 3 tablespoons chili to fill an 8-inch flour tortilla (you can also add a little grated Monterey Jack cheese). Put a little salsa in the bottom of a greased casserole dish and line up burritos next to one another. Top burritos with a little more salsa and some grated cheese, if desired. Bake at 350 degrees until cheese is melted, about 20 minutes. Serve with extra salsa, if desired.

Rice

More than half the world sustains itself on rice. From the short-grain Japanese sushi to the tantalizingly aromatic basmati of the Middle East, there is no end to the variety of this grain. No wonder millions of people can eat it day after day.

I grew up in a large family where rice was a common side dish, and there was little I liked better than a big pile of white rice with a pat of butter on the top. Sitting down to a meal the other night, my daughter exclaimed delightedly, "Rice and salad! Mmmmmmm. This is perfect, Mom!"

What a shame, then, that rice—particularly brown rice—became the very symbol of heavy, unappetizing vegetarian fare in this country. Instead of taking inspiration from the rice dishes of the 1960s, I look to other cultures to plumb the possibilities.

Common supermarket varieties—long-

and medium-grain—have been joined recently by rice mixes and varieties that vary meals without increasing preparation time. Pour homemade black bean gravy over preseasoned yellow-rice mix and it tastes entirely different than the same recipe made with long-grain rice. Dip into a barrel of organically grown rice mixes and specialty rices, such as wild rice and Texmati, and you'll realize you, too, could eat rice every day without becoming bored.

If you're a fan of brown rice but hate the extended cooking time, you can spend a little more for instant brown rice, which is ready in half the time. Or, if you are a good planner, try soaking regular brown rice in water overnight. For every 1 cup of rice, use 2 cups of water. When you're ready to cook it, drain the water, combine the rice with 2½ cups water and cook for 25 minutes. This technique saves about 20 minutes on the regular cooking time.

Don't get obsessive about thinking you need to eat brown rice to be healthy. Eating a lower-fat, plant-based diet with a lot of vegetables and grains is a tremendous step toward health. Choosing brown rice is a baby step in comparison.

r i c e

Rice Romanoff

THIS CHEESY DISH, A TAKEOFF ON NOODLES ROMANOFF, is seasoned with garlic and green onions. Low-fat cottage cheese stands in admirably for the sour cream traditionally used. The rice is topped with Cheddar cheese.

- **3 cups water**
- **1 teaspoon salt**
- **1½ cups long-grain white rice**
- **2 cups low-fat cottage cheese**
- **2-3 garlic cloves**
- **½ teaspoon freshly ground pepper**
- **3 green onions, trimmed**
- **1 cup grated Cheddar cheese**

After you blend the cheese, fill your blender container with soapy water and blend again. It expedites cleaning.

Preheat the oven to 375 degrees.

Bring water to a boil, adding ½ teaspoon salt. Add rice, stir once, then cover and reduce the heat to low. Cook for about 18 minutes, or until water is absorbed and rice is tender.

Meanwhile, place cottage cheese, garlic, pepper and remaining ½ teaspoon salt in a blender and blend until smooth. Mince green onions and add them to the blender. Combine rice, cottage cheese mixture and ¼ cup Cheddar cheese.

Butter an 8- or 9-inch square baking dish. Pour in rice mixture and scatter remaining ¾ cup Cheddar on top.

Bake for 20 minutes, or until casserole is heated through and cheese bubbles.

Serves 4. ~ Serve hot with a salad or broccoli, and rye or wheat rolls.

Aromatic Persian Rice

MY FAMILY LOVES this Middle-Eastern inspired combination of potatoes and mushrooms, delicately seasoned with basil and cinnamon. However strange it may sound, it's delicious.

- **3** **cups water**
- **1½** **cups long-grain white rice**
- **1** **teaspoon salt**
- **¼** **teaspoon cinnamon or a 2-inch cinnamon stick**
- **3** **medium baking potatoes**
- **¼** **cup olive oil or vegetable oil**
- **1** **medium onion, diced**
- **¼-½** **pound mushrooms**
- **½** **cup chopped fresh parsley, plus more for garnish**
- **1** **teaspoon dried basil**
- **Freshly ground pepper to taste**
- **¼** **cup tomato paste (½ of a 6-ounce can)**
- **Plain yogurt (optional)**

Freeze leftover tomato paste and use in other recipes like Vegetable-Bean Soup with Black Olives (page 46) or Curried Chick-Peas and Potatoes (page 82).

Bring water to a boil in a wide skillet or pan. Add rice, salt and cinnamon or cinnamon stick, stir once, then cover and reduce the heat to low. Cook for about 18 minutes, or until water is absorbed and rice is tender.

Meanwhile, peel potatoes, if desired, and cut into ½-inch dice. Heat oil in a wide, deep pot, such as a Dutch oven. Add potatoes and cook over high heat, stirring occasionally, for about 5 minutes.

Add onion to potatoes and cook until tender, about 10 minutes. Reduce the heat if vegetables seem to be burning, but you want crisp potatoes.

Clean mushrooms, cut into smallish chunks and add to the pan along with parsley, basil and pepper. Cook until mushrooms are heated through and shiny, about 5 minutes. Stir in tomato paste. Remove from the heat.

Add rice and toss gently to combine. Remove cinnamon stick, if using, before serving. Serve with plain yogurt on top, if desired, and sprinkle with extra parsley.

Serves 4 to 6. ~ Serve with tossed salad or squash cooked with dill.

Rice with Black-Eyed Peas

SOME PEOPLE CRAVE McDONALD'S when they leave home for too long and have to eat food they aren't accustomed to. In my case, it's a homey dish of beans and rice that I look forward to. This one is a perfect example because it's easy to assemble so it's immediately gratifying.

Black-eyed peas have a buttery texture. They are widely available in the South—canned, frozen and fresh in season.

Turmeric is a bright yellow spice that gives color to curry powder and ballpark mustard. Leftovers can be added in small amounts to other curried recipes in this book, such as Curried Potatoes and Eggplant (page 78).

- 1½ cups water
- ¾ cup long-grain white rice
- 1 tablespoon olive oil
- 1 small onion, diced
- ½-1 teaspoon turmeric
- ½ teaspoon salt
- ½ teaspoon freshly ground pepper
- ½ teaspoon cayenne or ½ minced jalapeño pepper (optional)
- 1 16-ounce can tomatoes, with juice
- 1 16-ounce can black-eyed peas

> You can serve the black-eyed peas as a sauce over the top of the rice and skip the baking stage altogether, which saves dirtying a casserole dish.

Preheat the oven to 350 degrees.

Bring water to a boil in a wide skillet or pan. Add rice, stir once, then cover and reduce the heat to low. Cook for about 18 minutes, or until water is absorbed and rice is tender.

Heat oil in a wide skillet over medium heat. Add onion and cook until just tender, about 10 minutes. Add turmeric, salt, pepper, cayenne or jalapeño (if using) and tomatoes, chopping them as you add them to the skillet. Add juice from the tomatoes and boil briefly. Drain the black-eyed peas and add them to the skillet.

Butter an 8-inch baking dish or 1½-quart soufflé dish. Place ½ of rice in the bottom, cover with ½ of bean mixture and top with a layer of remaining rice, then remaining bean mixture. (You can assemble the casserole ahead, cover and refrigerate for up to 2 days.)

Bake for 10 to 15 minutes, or for 40 minutes if the casserole has been refrigerated, until heated through. Serve hot.

Serves 3 to 4. ~ Serve with sliced, salted cucumbers stirred with yogurt or sour cream.

Savory Green Rice

THIS DISH IS PERFECT with spring and fall spinach, but it can also be made with Swiss chard and other midsummer greens. Leave out the fennel seeds if you don't like them, but I love the haunting, unusual flavor they give the rice. The amount of chopped spinach can be varied; 7 or 8 cups will work as well as the 6 cups called for here.

Please don't make this dish with Parmesan cheese from the cardboard cylinder box at the supermarket. Grating your own is what makes it exceptional. Or buy freshly grated cheese from the deli.

- 4 cups water
- 2 cups long-grain white rice
- 1 teaspoon salt
- 3 tablespoons olive oil or vegetable oil
- ¼ cup chopped pecans, pine nuts or nut of choice
- 3 large garlic cloves, minced
- 2 bunches fresh spinach, washed, stems removed and discarded, leaves chopped into thin strips (about 6 cups chopped), or two 10-ounce packages frozen spinach
- ½ teaspoon fennel seeds
- Pinch of grated nutmeg
- ½-1 cup grated Parmesan cheese

> This dish can be made with frozen spinach; buy whole leaves and chop them for the best texture.

Bring water to a boil in a wide skillet or pan. Add rice and salt, stir once, then cover and reduce the heat to low. Cook for about 18 minutes, or until water is absorbed and rice is tender.

Meanwhile, heat oil in a deep pot, such as a Dutch oven, and add nuts. Cook over medium

heat, stirring occasionally, until they begin to brown; add garlic. As soon as it begins to brown, about 3 minutes, add spinach a few handfuls at a time. Allow spinach to wilt as you stir, then add another few handfuls (if using frozen, chop it coarsely, partially thawing it if necessary). Add fennel seeds and nutmeg. When spinach is wilted (or heated through), add cooked rice and toss to mix.

Place in a large serving bowl, sprinkle with Parmesan cheese and serve. Pass more Parmesan at the table. Leftovers rewarm easily in a microwave or in a pan with a little water added.

Serves 4. ~ In the spring, serve with lettuce salad or asparagus. In the fall, serve with Sweet Potato Medallions (page 155).

Savory Green Rice with Dill and Feta

SPINACH, DILL AND FETA CHEESE is one of those combinations like chinos and white shirts: it always seems to work. Toss the mixture lightly when you combine it and, if you have young diners, consider omitting the red pepper.

3 cups water
1½ cups long-grain white rice
1 teaspoon salt
3 garlic cloves
3 tablespoons olive oil
1 10-ounce package frozen chopped spinach, thawed
Freshly ground pepper to taste
1 teaspoon dried dill
¼ teaspoon hot red pepper flakes, or to taste
4 ounces feta cheese, crumbled (about ¾ cup)

Bring water to a boil in a wide skillet or medium pan over high heat. Add rice and salt, stir once, then cover and reduce the heat to low. Simmer for 18 minutes, or until water is absorbed and rice is tender.

Meanwhile, mince garlic. Combine it with oil in a wide skillet and cook over medium-high heat for 1 minute, or until softened. Squeeze spinach to remove excess water and add to the skillet, breaking it up with a fork. Add pepper, dill and red pepper flakes and heat through.

When rice is cooked, toss it gently with spinach mixture, then stir in feta cheese. Serve hot.

Serves 4 to 6. ~ Serve with grated peeled beets seasoned with Honey-Mustard Vinaigrette (page 16).

Mexican Rice

CASSEROLES ARE LIKE STATION WAGONS: sturdy, dependable, functional. They aren't the cusp of the next trend, but they make your life easier. This casserole can be prepared ahead, even frozen, then heated when you need it. It travels to potlucks, becomes a reliable part of a buffet and can be reheated by children in the microwave. To zip it up, add slices of pickled jalapeño.

- **2 cups water**
- **1 teaspoon salt**
- **1 cup long-grain white rice**
- **1 cup low-fat cottage cheese**
- **1 4-ounce can chopped mild green chilies**
- **1 4-ounce jar chopped pimiento**
- **½-1 teaspoon chili powder**
- **Few drops hot red pepper sauce, or to taste**
- **1 cup grated Monterey Jack cheese (about 4 ounces)**

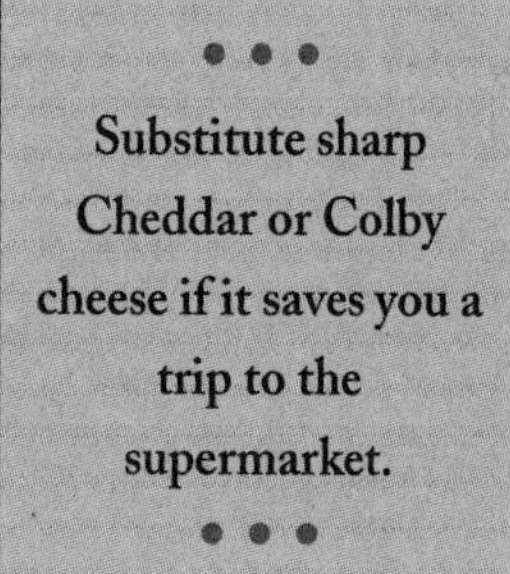

Preheat the oven to 400 degrees.

Bring water to a boil, adding salt. Add rice, stir once, then cover and reduce the heat to low. Cook for about 18 minutes, or until water is absorbed and rice is tender.

Meanwhile, blend cottage cheese in a blender. Add green chilies, pimiento, chili powder and hot sauce. Stir with a spoon. Stir into hot rice. Pour into a buttered casserole or soufflé dish and top with grated cheese.

Bake for 20 minutes, or until cheese is bubbly and casserole is heated through.

Serves 4 as a main dish. ~ Serve with sliced tomatoes or salad and a side dish of pinto beans seasoned with garlic and jalapeño pepper.

Spicy Fried Rice

ONCE YOU'RE COMFORTABLE making fried rice, you'll have an easy, nutritious and filling dinner at your fingertips. Use this recipe as a guide and substitute other seasonal vegetables that you have on hand. First you add aromatics to the wok (onion, garlic and hot pepper, but it could easily be green onions and ginger). Then you add the vegetables, the firmest ones first, the tenderest last. Next you stir in cooked rice and heat it through, and finally you season it with soy sauce.

- 4 cups cooked long-grain white rice or 2 cups uncooked
- 4 cups water (if using uncooked rice)
- 1 teaspoon salt (if using uncooked rice)
- 2 tablespoons vegetable oil
- 1 medium onion, peeled and thinly sliced
- 2 garlic cloves, minced
- 1 hot pepper (such as jalapeño), minced
- 1 bell pepper, cored and cut into small chunks
- 2 medium carrots, peeled and diced
- 2 6-inch zucchini, washed and diced
- ½ cup water or vegetable broth (if using leftover rice)
- Soy sauce and freshly ground pepper to taste

• • •

To make the dish faster and easier, use leftover rice and frozen mixed vegetables.

• • •

If you don't have leftover rice, bring water to a boil, adding salt. Add rice, stir once, then cover and reduce the heat to low. Cook for about 18 minutes, or until water is absorbed and rice is tender. Set aside.

Heat a wok, wide skillet or Dutch oven over high heat (if your skillet is nonstick or coated with enamel, heat it for only a few seconds). When it is hot, add oil, then onion. Cook, stirring, for 2 minutes, or until they just begin to color. Add garlic and hot peppers. Stir once.

Add bell peppers and carrots and cook, stirring, for 2 minutes. Add zucchini and cook for 2 minutes more, stirring constantly, until the vegetables are evenly cooked.

Add rice (if adding leftover rice, add water or vegetable broth) and stir to combine. Season with soy sauce and lots of pepper.

Serves 4 generously. ~ Serve with a bowl of fruit in season—oranges in winter, peaches in summer, apples in fall.

Vietnamese Fried Rice

WHILE THE FOLLOWING INGREDIENT LIST looks long, the preparation of this rice is simple. Prepare the soy mixture, cook the eggs, prepare the vegetables, then toss everything with rice. You can omit the eggs if you wish, but they are savory little nuggets of flavor that make the dish that much more appealing.

- 4-5 cups cooked long-grain white rice or 2 cups uncooked
- 4 cups water (if using uncooked rice)
- ¾ teaspoon salt (if using uncooked rice)
- ¼ cup soy sauce
- 1 tablespoon sugar
- 1 teaspoon hot red pepper sauce, or to taste
- 3 large eggs (or 6 egg whites)
- Salt
- 5 tablespoons vegetable oil
- 1 bunch green onions, trimmed and chopped
- 4 garlic cloves, minced
- 2 cups shredded cabbage (any kind)
- 2 carrots, peeled and chopped
- ½ cup water or vegetable broth (if using leftover rice)
- Fresh cilantro, minced

• • •

Cilantro (also called coriander or Chinese parsley) is critical to dishes from Southeast Asia, but if you don't like it, leave it out.

• • •

If you don't have leftover rice, bring water to a boil, adding ½ teaspoon salt. Add rice, stir once, then cover and reduce the heat to low. Cook for about 18 minutes, or until water is absorbed and rice is tender. Set aside.

Combine soy sauce, sugar and red pepper sauce in a bowl.

Beat eggs in another bowl with remaining ¼ teaspoon salt. Heat a cast-iron skillet or wok over high heat for 2 minutes (if your skillet is nonstick or coated with enamel, heat it for only a few seconds). Add 2 tablespoons oil and half the chopped green onions. Pour in eggs and cook, tipping the wok or skillet back and forth as you stir intermittently, until they have set, about 2 minutes. Transfer to a large platter and set aside.

Add 2 tablespoons oil to the pan and add remaining green onions and garlic. Cook, stirring, for 30 seconds. Add cabbage and carrots and cook, stirring, for 2 minutes. Transfer to the platter with the eggs.

Add remaining 1 tablespoon oil to the skillet and add rice. If you are using leftover rice, add water or vegetable broth—don't add water if rice is freshly cooked. Add soy sauce mixture and stir to coat.

Toss eggs, vegetables and rice together and serve, topped with cilantro.

Serves 4 generously. ~ This recipe is complemented by fruit in season—oranges in winter, peaches in summer, pears in fall.

Cajun Beans and Rice

TRADITIONALLY, CAJUN RED BEANS are cooked with a ham bone (or other pork) and served like gravy over a mound of rice. It's a delicious combination designed to stretch resources to the maximum—what a women's magazine might call a budget dish. But you can make it without ham by substituting a flavorful combination of vegetables, herbs, salt and pepper. The amount of cayenne called for is just right, but if you're cooking for children, you might want to cut down on it a bit.

Use dried thyme leaves for this dish, not powdered thyme, which loses flavor quickly as it's stored and can taste medicinal if you use too much.

- 2 tablespoons vegetable oil
- 1 medium onion, chopped
- 2 garlic cloves, minced
- 1 green bell pepper, cored and chopped
- 1 celery rib, finely chopped
- 1½ teaspoons dried thyme leaves
- ½ teaspoon cayenne (or ½ minced jalapeño pepper), or to taste
- 3 cups water or vegetable broth (or a combination)
- 1½ cups long-grain white rice
- ½ teaspoon salt
- Freshly ground pepper to taste
- 1 16-ounce can red beans (2 cups cooked)

• • •

Canned vegetable broth usually comes in 2-cup cans. Avoid leftovers in this recipe by using 1 can plus 1 cup water.

• • •

Heat oil in a large saucepan. Add onion, garlic, green pepper, celery, thyme and cayenne. Cook over high heat until tender, stirring often to prevent burning, 5 to 10 minutes. If you add the vegetables one at a time as you prepare them, keep the heat on medium or medium-high, then turn it up to high when you are free to stir the mixture often.

Stir in water or broth and rice, salt and some pepper. Stir once. Bring to a boil and cover, reduce the heat to low and cook for about 18 minutes, until rice is tender.

Add beans and stir very gently to mix. Heat for 1 to 2 minutes, or until beans are hot. Serve immediately.

Serves 4. ~ Serve with baked butternut squash in winter, salad in spring and fall, sliced tomatoes in summer.

Greek Rice

WHEN YOUR ENTHUSIASM FOR COOKING EBBS, try this dish, which takes little effort. Artichoke hearts improve the flavor of nearly any dish; here, they are complemented by lemon and parsley. You'll like the meal best if you use fresh parsley and freshly squeezed lemon juice. If you prefer, serve the topping over pasta instead of rice. You can also substitute freshly grated Parmesan or Asiago cheese for the feta.

- 3 cups water
- 1 teaspoon salt
- 1½ cups long-grain white rice
- 2 6-ounce jars marinated artichoke hearts
- 1 14-ounce can diced tomatoes, with juice
- ¼ cup sliced black olives (canned is fine, but drain them)
- ½ cup chopped fresh parsley
- 1 teaspoon dried oregano
- Juice of 1 lemon
- Freshly ground pepper
- 1 cup feta cheese

> Substitute fresh tomatoes for canned, if you have them.

Bring water to a boil, adding salt. Add rice, stir once, then cover and reduce the heat to low. Cook for about 18 minutes, or until water is absorbed and rice is tender. Fluff with a fork.

Meanwhile, reserving the liquid from the jars, chop artichoke hearts into small pieces and combine in a pan or skillet with the artichoke liquid, tomatoes and juices, olives, parsley, oregano, lemon juice and pepper. Bring to a boil, then reduce the heat to low and simmer, breaking up a few of the larger tomato chunks.

When rice is cooked, serve on 4 plates, topped with artichoke mixture and sprinkled with feta cheese.

Serves 4. ~ Serve with rolls and corn on the cob in summer, Roasted Honey-Mustard Carrots (page 153) in winter.

Potatoes

POTATOES PLAY a central role in vegetarian cuisine. My children's favorite meal is potato chunks sautéed in a skillet so they are partly browned, served with cooked broccoli and cheese sauce. They'd eat it every day if they could and frankly, so would I.

But then I'd miss one of my favorite dishes of all time: Greek Potatoes—browned potatoes flavored with liberal amounts of cooked onion, fresh parsley, tomatoes and olives (page 80). Or Curried Potatoes and Eggplant (page 78)—a time-honored combination that opens the door to exploring other India-inspired foods. Or a deceptively simple but delicious Warm Potato Salad (page 83), which, though it seems like a side dish, always upstages anything else on the plate. All of these are filling crossover meals that you can serve to people who might otherwise be suspicious of vegetarian food.

For baking and frying, the best potato is the widely available Idaho russet baking

potato, found in net bags piled high in the supermarket produce section. Virtually all of them weigh between 5½ and 7 ounces and—during sales—cost as little as 9 cents per pound. They are a nutritional bargain, loaded with vitamin C, protein, B vitamins, potassium, iron and fiber, with each one contributing less than 150 calories.

The waxy, firmer-fleshed potatoes—the kind we call "new" when they are golf-ball size and refer to as "boiling" potatoes when they are bigger—are more suitable than russets for boiling and slicing into salad. They hold their shape a little better when you slice and stir them. Also, their firm texture resists absorbing tons of fatty dressing, so you don't need to add as much.

For hurried cooks, the thin skins of boiling potatoes are a boon. They don't need peeling. Once the potatoes have cooled enough to handle, just slice them.

Unfortunately, the densely fleshed potato is one food that perpetuates the stereotype that vegetarian food takes time to prepare. It's true that they benefit from long cooking, but knowing a few time-saving tricks can help you get them to the table quickly:

- Use the microwave, which can cook potato flesh faster than conducted or convected heat can. Microwaves cannot brown, but they can help speed the process. Cube the potatoes, microwave them for a few minutes, then fry them in a skillet with a little olive oil and minced onion.

  You can also precook the potatoes in water, which takes a little longer and requires another pot.

- Whenever you bake or boil potatoes, cook a few extra to use later in dishes like home fries.

- Simmer potatoes in a covered pot rather than baking them. The heat from a simmering liquid penetrates the potato sooner than the hot air of an oven.

- Bake sliced potatoes in a thin layer in a wide baking dish rather than stacking them in a casserole, so the heat doesn't have as far to penetrate and the potatoes cook quickly.

potatoes

Dusted Potatoes

Because these potatoes require almost no effort, you can spend a little more time on another accompaniment or two and have a wonderful meal. This dish is all the more appealing because you are likely to have all the ingredients for it on your shelf.

4 medium potatoes
1 tablespoon olive oil
1 teaspoon paprika
½ teaspoon salt
½ teaspoon freshly ground pepper
Pinch cayenne
Pinch ground nutmeg

> **You don't have to premix the spices before sprinkling them on the potatoes, but they'll spread more evenly if you do.**

Preheat the oven to 375 degrees.

Lightly grease a wide, shallow baking pan (a 15-by-11-inch pan is good) with oil. Wash potatoes, peel, if desired, and cut into 1-inch chunks. Put potatoes on the baking pan, drizzle with oil and toss with your fingers to coat them.

Combine paprika, salt, pepper, cayenne and nutmeg in a small bowl and sprinkle over potatoes.

Bake for 20 minutes, stirring once or twice, until potatoes are brown on some sides and tender. Serve immediately.

Serves 4. ~ These are good with nearly any vegetable side dish—Marinated Green Beans (page 23) or chopped cooked spinach seasoned with horseradish and a little sour cream. Serve with applesauce and rolls.

Speedy Baked Potatoes

BAKED POTATOES ARE FUNDAMENTAL to the diet of a vegetarian. They can be eaten plain, salted, sour-creamed, filled with salsa or topped with broccoli and black olives, with any variation on a pasta sauce or with stewed vegetables.

Unfortunately, the best baked potato is achieved through slow cooking. When baked at 350 degrees for 1¼ hours, the skin becomes thick, chewy and dry, with a nice brown layer under the skin that adds loads of flavor. Cut the potato, open it to let the steam escape, and it will have perfect, fluffy dry flesh.

Because great potatoes take so long to bake, you might try pairing microwaving with conventional baking. Microwaving gets the potato started, and the oven finishes the job and gives the potatoes that dry skin and brown flavor everyone loves.

4 medium potatoes

A 5½-to-7-ounce potato (from those net bags in the supermarket) requires about 2 minutes to cook halfway in the microwave on high power. For each additional potato, add another 2 minutes. Total microwave time for 4 medium potatoes is 8 minutes. Be sure to puncture the potatoes before microwaving them so they don't burst, and rearrange them once during cooking.

Meanwhile, preheat the oven to 450 degrees. When potatoes have been microwaved, bake them for 20 minutes, or until the flesh is soft when you insert a sharp knife into it. Split potatoes, open them wide and serve immediately for the fluffiest flesh.

If you change the number or the size of potatoes you microwave, you'll need to adjust the microwave time.

Suggested Toppings for Baked Potatoes

- Salsa: homemade or from the supermarket. Add sour cream or avocado chunks, if you like.
- Spaghetti sauce: homemade or from the supermarket. Sprinkle with grated mozzarella or provolone cheese, if desired.
- Fresh mushrooms, sliced and cooked in garlic butter.
- Broccoli in cheese sauce: Combine 2 tablespoons butter and 2 tablespoons flour in a small saucepan and stir in 1 cup milk; cook until thickened. Stir in 1 cup sharp Cheddar cheese. Or broccoli sautéed in olive oil with garlic and black olives.
- Capers and a little of their brine.
- Fresh, peeled tomatoes cooked in olive oil with garlic and artichoke hearts.
- A sprinkling of crumbled blue, feta or Gorgonzola cheese.
- Cottage cheese mixed with dill or fresh chives (or minced green onions) or both. Blend the cottage cheese in the blender until smooth.

Curried Potatoes and Eggplant

EGGPLANT AND POTATOES are often combined in Indian cuisine. Not only do they taste good together, but they are also ready in the garden at the same time. Season them with a mixture of curry spices, and you have a satisfying dinner.

When you're buying fresh ginger, break off what you need and just buy that. If you do buy more than you need, keep it at room temperature (not in the refrigerator, where it will dry out more quickly) or freeze it for longer storage.

- 1 8-inch-long eggplant
- 1 teaspoon salt, plus more to taste
- 3 tablespoons olive oil or vegetable oil
- 4 large garlic cloves, minced
- 1 tablespoon peeled, minced fresh ginger
- 2 teaspoons ground cumin
- 1 teaspoon ground coriander
- 1 medium onion, sliced
- 1½ pounds potatoes, peeled and cubed
- Freshly ground pepper to taste
- 8 ounces plain nonfat yogurt (optional)

Peel eggplant, cut into 1-inch cubes and place in a colander. Sprinkle with salt, toss briefly and set in the sink to drain.

Heat oil in a Dutch oven over high heat. Add garlic, ginger, cumin and coriander. Cook, stirring, for about 30 seconds, then add onion. Cook on high heat, stirring occasionally, until it begins to brown; add potatoes.

Rinse eggplant and lift out a handful of cubes. Press your hands firmly together to squeeze juice out of cubes—press as hard as you can. Add cubes to potatoes and stir, then repeat with remaining eggplant. Cover, reduce the heat to medium-low and cook for 15 minutes, stirring occasionally, adjusting the heat as necessary, until potatoes are cooked. If not, cook for another 10 minutes, or until potatoes and eggplant are quite tender.

Season with salt and pepper. Serve hot, topped with yogurt, if desired.

Serves 6 to 8. ~ Serve with warm pita bread and a cool raw vegetable, such as sliced tomatoes and cucumbers.

Variation

Hot Potatoes and Eggplant: Add a minced jalapeño pepper—or your favorite hot pepper in an amount to suit your taste—when you add the potatoes.

You can add chopped tomatoes to this dish after the potatoes have cooked. Use 2 to 3 medium fresh tomatoes, chopped, or 1½ cups chopped cherry tomatoes or a 16-ounce can of whole tomatoes, with juice, cut into small pieces.

Greek Potatoes

GARDENERS WHO COOK seasonally sometimes complain that, come February, there's nothing to eat but potatoes and onions. This stew glorifies the two.

You can make the entire dish in one pan, but I choose to speed the process by letting the potatoes bake in the oven while I prepare the rest of the dish on the stove. If you want to save on cleanup and can spare the time, start the dish by cooking all the onions in the olive oil until they are quite limp, then put in the potatoes and brown them over medium-high heat, stirring. Add the tomatoes only when the potatoes are nearly tender, as the acid in the tomato juice slows the cooking time.

- ¼ cup olive oil
- 5 medium potatoes, peeled and cubed
- 3 medium onions, thickly sliced
- 3-4 garlic cloves, minced
- 1 jalapeño pepper, seeded and minced, or ½ teaspoon crushed red pepper (optional)
- 1 16-ounce can tomatoes, coarsely chopped, with juice
- ½ cup coarsely chopped imported black olives or stuffed green olives
- 2-3 ounces feta cheese, crumbled (½-¾ cup)

A cherry-pitting gadget makes it easy to pit imported black olives, but you can pit them with a paring knife.

Preheat the oven to 350 degrees.

Heat 2 tablespoons oil in a wide, heavy cast-iron skillet. Add potatoes and cook over high heat (if the oil begins to spit wildly, you can turn the heat down a little), stirring until the potatoes get crisp and brown, about 10 minutes in all. Place in the oven.

Heat remaining 2 tablespoons oil in a Dutch oven. Add onions, garlic and jalapeño if using (add crushed red pepper later, if using) and cook over high heat, stirring often, until onions begin to brown.

Add tomatoes, mincing them well as you do. Add juice from the can, olives and crushed red pepper, if using. Stir in potatoes and cook until they are fully tender. Serve topped with feta cheese.

Serves 4. ~ Serve with salad or green beans.

Curried Chick-Peas and Potatoes

THIS THICK AND CHUNKY chick-pea and potato stew gets a curried flavor from ginger and cumin. If you like heat, add some fresh jalapeño or hot pepper of choice. If you don't like cilantro, leave it out.

- 2-3 tablespoons butter or vegetable oil
- 2 tablespoons peeled, minced fresh ginger
- 2 large onions
- 1 4-ounce can chopped mild green chilies
- 1 16-ounce can chick-peas (also called garbanzo beans)
- 1 teaspoon ground cumin
- 2 medium potatoes
- ¼ cup tomato paste (½ of a 6-ounce can)
- Salt and freshly ground black pepper to taste
- ⅓-½ cup minced fresh cilantro
- Plain low-fat yogurt (optional)

• • •

Freeze the remaining can of tomato paste and use it in Vegetable-Bean Soup with Black Olives (page 46) or Cauliflower with Long Noodles.

• • •

Heat butter or oil in a Dutch oven or other wide, deep pan over medium heat, add ginger and fry it as you peel and slice onions about ¼ inch thick. Add onions to the pan and increase the heat to high. Stir often and cook until light brown. Add green chilies, chick-peas and cumin.

You can adjust the heat as you peel potatoes, but keep it as high as you can without burning the mixture, stirring occasionally. Cut potatoes into 1-inch squares, add to pan, cover and cook, stirring occasionally, for 30 minutes, or until potatoes are nearly tender. Add tomato paste and cook for 10 minutes more. Season with salt and pepper. Serve topped with minced cilantro and yogurt, if desired.

Serves 4. ~ Serve with peeled and seeded cucumber, cut into chunks, salted and dressed with yogurt or sour cream.

Warm Potato Salad

IF YOU'VE BEEN TAPPED for a company or school potluck, consider taking these potatoes. They're familiar enough to be tried, delicious enough to be loved.

They started out as an accompaniment, but they taste so good that everybody takes seconds, so I always serve them as a main dish.

- 8 medium potatoes
- 1 cup minced fresh parsley
- 2 garlic cloves, minced
- ¼ cup olive oil or vegetable oil
- 2 tablespoons vinegar (any kind)
- ½ jalapeño pepper, minced
- ¼ teaspoon grated nutmeg
- 1 teaspoon salt
- ½ teaspoon freshly ground pepper

> This recipe makes a lot, so I take leftovers to lunch or reheat them for dinner the next day. If you don't carry your lunch, cut the recipe in half.

Quarter potatoes and place in a large pot of boiling water. Lower the heat and simmer until tender, about 15 to 20 minutes.

Meanwhile, place parsley and garlic in a small jar or bowl. Add oil, vinegar, jalapeño, nutmeg, salt and pepper. Screw the lid on the jar and shake vigorously or beat with a fork to dissolve salt.

Drain potatoes and, when they are just cool enough to handle, cut them into chunks. Put them in a serving bowl and drizzle with dressing. Serve hot, warm or at room temperature.

Serves 6 generously. ~ Serve with a green salad in spring and fall, red cabbage in winter, Greek Peasant Salad (page 20) in summer.

Cabbage and Potatoes

I DIDN'T COME TO CABBAGE AND POTATOES until late in life. The combination is firmly entrenched in many cuisines, including Italian. It is surprisingly sweet, so I like to sprinkle the dish with an aged sharp cheese, such as provolone or fontina.

2 tablespoons olive oil or vegetable oil
1 medium onion, chopped
2 teaspoons ground cumin
About 6 cups shredded cabbage
3 medium potatoes
1 teaspoon salt
½ teaspoon freshly ground pepper
1-2 cups grated fontina or provolone cheese

> **If you like to avoid the fat in cheese, you might want to add a few minced olives or capers instead.**

Heat oil in a wide, deep pan, such as a Dutch oven. Add onion and cumin and cook over high heat, stirring occasionally, until onions are soft. Add cabbage and cook, stirring occasionally, as you prepare potatoes.

Peel and dice potatoes into ½-inch cubes (don't worry about the size, but the smaller the cube, the faster it cooks). Add potatoes, along with salt and pepper. Stir occasionally as cabbage cooks down and potatoes get brown, about 30 minutes. Top with cheese and serve.

Serves 4. ~ Serve hot with rolls and tossed salad or sliced mushrooms marinated in Honey-Mustard Vinaigrette (page 16).

Artichoke and Potato Stew

When you want something a little elegant, try this stew. Tarragon and artichoke hearts make it unusual and delicious. Would fresh artichoke hearts taste better? Of course! And cleaning them would be an excellent occupation for teenagers. But if you lack time and teenagers, frozen work fine; canned would be the last choice.

2 tablespoons olive oil
2 medium onions, diced
2 large garlic cloves, minced
1 medium carrot, diced
3 large potatoes
3-4 cups artichoke hearts (two 9-ounce packages, frozen)
2 cups (1 can) vegetable stock or water
1 teaspoon dried tarragon
1 teaspoon dried thyme leaves
Salt and freshly ground pepper to taste

Heat oil in a wide, deep pot, such as a Dutch oven. Add onions and cook over medium-high heat, stirring occasionally, until they begin to brown, about 10 minutes.

Add garlic, cook for 30 seconds, stirring, then add carrot. Peel potatoes and cut into ½-inch dice, adding them to the pot as you do. Add artichoke hearts, vegetable stock or water, tarragon, thyme, salt and pepper.

Bring to a boil, reduce the heat to low, cover and simmer until potatoes are soft, about 20 minutes. Ladle into soup bowls and serve.

Serves 4 to 6. ~ Serve with French rolls that have been split, buttered, toasted and sprinkled with Parmesan cheese.

Potato Pizza Casserole

THIS DISH USES POTATOES instead of bread as a "crust," then relies on the usual suspects—mushrooms, tomato sauce, garlic and oregano—to get a pizza theme going. The casserole bakes faster if you microwave the potato slices before you bake them, but if you don't have a microwave, you can still make the dish. Just cook the potatoes longer in the final baking stage.

About 1½ pounds potatoes (5 medium)
3 tablespoons olive oil
Salt and freshly ground pepper
1 garlic clove, minced
½ pound fresh mushrooms, cleaned and sliced
1 teaspoon dried thyme leaves
½ teaspoon dried oregano
1 8-ounce can tomato sauce
1-2 cups grated aged sharp cheese, such as Asiago, Cheddar or a mixture
¼-½ cup chopped pitted imported black olives

For a Mexican casserole, use store-bought enchilada sauce instead of tomato sauce, season the mushrooms with ground cumin and sprinkle the dish with hot pepper cheese (Monterey Jack studded with bits of jalapeño).

Preheat the oven to 400 degrees. Wash potatoes and slice them ¼ inch thick. To speed things along, you can put them in a microwave-safe container. Cover with plastic wrap, turn back a corner to let steam escape and microwave on high power for 10 minutes, or until potatoes are barely tender. Set aside.

Generously grease an 11-by-15-inch shallow baking pan with 1 tablespoon oil. Arrange potato slices so they are overlapping in the pan and sprinkle with salt and pepper. Bake for 15 to 20 minutes while you prepare toppings.

Heat remaining 2 tablespoons oil in a wide skillet. Add garlic and cook for several seconds, stirring, until it is aromatic, then add mushrooms, thyme and oregano. Cook until mushrooms have shrunk somewhat, about 10 minutes.

After potatoes have cooked for about 15 to 20 minutes, remove them from the oven, pour tomato sauce over them, then sprinkle with mushroom mixture. Sprinkle with cheese, then olives. Bake for 15 minutes more, or until potatoes are tender and cheese is melted and bubbly. Or, if you have not microwaved potatoes, bake for 25 minutes more, or until potatoes are tender. Serve hot.

Serves 4. ~ Serve with salad or a green vegetable, such as steamed broccoli or stir-fried green beans.

Potatoes au Gratin

POTATOES AU GRATIN is one of those American casseroles that tastes fabulous and takes forever to cook. That's why it's more a fixture of our memories than our dinner tables.

I use a few trusted techniques to quicken the pace. High temperatures cook the potatoes faster, and instead of layering them in a deep casserole, I spread them out in a wide one so the heat can get to all of them at once. You can hurry things along even further by warming the milk in your microwave or a small pan before you add it to the potatoes. If you have the time, lower the heat to 350 degrees and bake these potatoes for an hour or more.

This dish is a great place to use little ends of cheese you might have, so don't run to the store for sharp Cheddar if you have a little bit of provolone or Monterey Jack and a few sprinkles of Parmesan. Potatoes love any kind of cheese. Also, I use skim milk in this dish and it works fine.

2 pounds potatoes, peeled and sliced ⅛ inch thick
Salt and freshly ground pepper to taste
2 garlic cloves, minced (optional)
1 cup grated sharp Cheddar cheese
1 cup milk

Lots of black pepper makes this dish taste exceptional. Don't skimp.

Preheat the oven to 425 degrees. Lightly grease a 9-by-13-inch baking pan or similar wide casserole.

Overlap potato slices in a single layer in the pan. Sprinkle with salt and pepper, then scatter garlic, if using, and cheese over top. Pour milk over all and bake for 40 minutes, or until potatoes are tender. The dish should be dry, not saucy.

Serves 4 to 6. ~ Serve with Sweet-and-Sour Cucumber Salad (page 27) or a green salad and fried or fresh apple slices.

Potatoes and Blue Cheese

THIS WARM POTATO SALAD is dressed with a thin, vinegary dressing rather than mayonnaise. It is similar to German potato salad, but I substitute blue cheese for the bacon in the original. A lot of people can't identify the flavor, but they love it just the same.

- **1½ pounds small or medium-size waxy potatoes (such as red-skinned), left whole**
- **5 tablespoons olive oil**
- **1 bunch green onions, trimmed**
- **2 tablespoons vinegar (apple cider is good, but any kind will do)**
- **Salt and freshly ground pepper**
- **2 celery ribs, chopped (about 1 cup)**
- **4-6 ounces blue cheese (about 1 cup crumbled)**

> **Either walnut-size new potatoes or medium-size potatoes work here; adjust your cooking time accordingly.**

Cook potatoes in boiling water until tender when pierced with a paring knife, about 30 minutes for medium-size potatoes. Drain and set aside to cool briefly.

Meanwhile, heat oil in a small skillet. Mince green onions and add them to the skillet. Cook briefly over medium heat, just to soften onions, about 3 minutes. Remove from the heat.

When potatoes are just cool enough to handle, cut them into bite-size pieces. Toss them in a medium-size bowl with vinegar. Season generously with salt and pepper and toss again. Drizzle with onion-oil mixture and toss to coat, then add celery and blue cheese and toss gently. Serve hot, warm or at room temperature.

Serves 4 to 6. ~ Serve with Barbecued Black-Eyed Peas (page 121) and Sweet-and-Sour Cucumber Salad (page 27) or sliced tomatoes.

Pasta

GREAT PASTA is great food, period. No apologies. Nearly everybody likes it. And don't let the food snobs pull the wool over your eyes—dried pasta is fabulous, and if you don't think the Italians rely on it more than we do, check out any Italian supermarket. Fresh pasta has its virtues, but dried is preferable in the recipes that follow.

Far too many words have been written about pairing the right pasta with the right sauce. The result has draped a haze of uncertainty over pasta cookery: Average home cooks approach it with more trepidation than pleasure. Instead, we should develop our own preferences through experience. All we need to know is what we like. I guarantee you that nobody will ever leave your dinner party snorting, "Well, can you imagine serving greens and olives with *rotini*!"

Many of us grew up eating the faithful

standards: spaghetti with red sauce (with or without meat) and macaroni and cheese. But pasta offers vegetarians much more. It adds dignity to what might otherwise be called leftovers. Leftover cooked broccoli heated in a skillet with garlic, olive oil and red pepper flakes and tossed with pasta is a whole new meal.

Exploit the ease with which pasta can become dinner. Boiling water is about all that's needed. Then you can heat some diced tomatoes in the microwave with dried basil, oregano and black pepper. Or cook white beans with loads of fresh parsley and chopped green olives and serve over noodles with cheese.

If there is a challenge to pasta, it's in the cooking—finding that ever elusive al dente stage so popular with recipe writers all over the country. Cooking pasta past al dente—firm and chewy—doesn't mean you're a bad cook; you'll just get more pleasure (and more satisfaction) from pasta that's cooked chewy rather than mushy. Al dente pasta does interesting things inside your mouth. The texture is noticeable and complements whatever accompanies it—soft fried zucchini or smooth tomato sauce. Contrasting texture is one of the benchmarks of good cooking, and, in this case, it's also the fastest method.

The pasta should be firm when the diner takes his first bite. If it is barely firm when it comes out of the water, it will be overdone by the time it arrives at the table. If the noodles are to be cooked after they are boiled, say, stirred in a skillet with vegetables and broth, they should be quite firm—that is, perceptibly crunchy—when they come out of the pot.

Judging the proper timing depends on the type of noodle and how quickly your water returns to a boil (large pots take longer than smaller ones to boil initially but quickly return to the boil once the noodles are added). If you're cooking dried noodles that you bought at the supermarket, read the directions on the package and start tasting the noodles at half the suggested cooking time.

pasta

Pasta Estivi

Estivi means "summer" in Italian, and that's when this dish tastes best. If your garden (or your neighbor's) is overrun with tomatoes, you'll appreciate having this recipe. The sweet tanginess of perfect tomatoes, in combination with the vinegar, makes a refreshing and surprising topping for hot pasta.

2 cups chopped tomatoes or halved cherry tomatoes
1 bunch green onions, trimmed and chopped
3 tablespoons olive oil
1 tablespoon vinegar (any kind)
Freshly ground pepper and salt
8 ounces rotini (corkscrew) noodles
½-1 cup crumbled blue cheese
1 tablespoon chopped fresh herb (basil, mint, thyme, oregano) or 1 tablespoon chopped fresh parsley mixed with ½ teaspoon dried basil

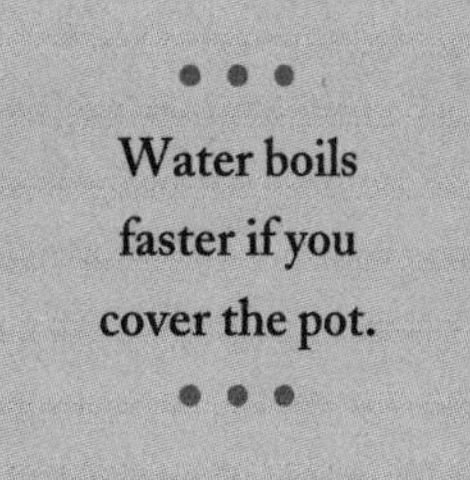

Combine tomatoes (peel only if desired and don't peel cherry tomatoes) with green onions, oil, vinegar and pepper to taste. Season with salt to taste and chill.

Cook noodles in boiling water for about 10 minutes, or until done to desired taste. Drain, shake to remove excess water and place in a broad bowl or platter. Top with tomato mixture, crumbled cheese and herbs and serve.

Serves 4. ~ Serve with green beans sautéed with garlic.

Pasta with White Beans and Tomatoes

WHITE BEANS AND PASTA are ideal partners. In this dish, the beans add satisfying substance to a conventional tomato sauce that gets its fresh taste from parsley, which is easily found at the supermarket. If you have fresh basil and/or oregano in your garden, by all means add some to the sauce.

- ¼ cup olive oil
- 4 large garlic cloves, minced
- 2 14½-ounce cans stewed tomatoes or one 28-ounce can diced or crushed tomatoes in juice
- ½ cup chopped fresh parsley, plus more for garnish
- 1 teaspoon dried oregano
- 1 16-ounce can white beans (such as Great Northern)
- ¼ cup chopped imported black olives or stuffed green olives
- Freshly ground pepper and salt to taste
- 12 ounces linguine or fettuccine
- 4-6 ounces feta cheese (about 1 cup crumbled)

> You can substitute Parmesan or Cheddar for the feta. Grate it coarsely for a more interesting texture.

Heat oil in a wide skillet over medium-high heat. Add garlic and cook for 1 minute, or until aromatic. Add tomatoes, parsley and oregano. Simmer for about 10 minutes, or until mixture has thickened considerably. Lower the heat if mixture is spitting violently. Add white beans and olives and cook, stirring, to heat through. Add pepper and salt—but remember, the feta will be quite salty.

As the mixture cooks, bring a large pot of water to a boil, add pasta and cook for about 9 minutes, or until barely tender. Drain and toss with pasta sauce. The sauce has excess liquid, so pasta should be slightly undercooked. It will cook further in the hot sauce and absorb some of it. Serve sprinkled with feta cheese and more parsley.

Serves 4 to 6. ~ Serve with green beans or Savory Broccoli Salad (page 28).

Simple Lo Mein

Before you decide not to make this dish because it contains kohlrabi, let me assure you that you can substitute other vegetables that can be cut into matchsticks, including broccoli stems or cabbage, and it will be delicious. I suggest kohlrabi because it's a winter vegetable, because it's good for you, and because this is an excellent place to introduce yourself to it. My kids eat kohlrabi without knowing it.

Kohlrabi looks like it comes from Mars, with leaves growing on stems that come out of the sides of the bulbous root like so many arms. But it looks far stranger than it tastes. It most closely resembles the firm texture and flavor of broccoli stems or a very mild turnip. Trim the stems and peel the skin (both with a paring knife) and you'll have a round vegetable that's easy to cut into slivers. Shave off a slice to create a flat side so it stays steady, then slice it in ¼-inch slices. Stack the slices in two or three stacks and cut down to make matchsticks.

This dish is also good with a dash of hot pepper sauce.

- 8 ounces fettuccine
- 3 tablespoons vegetable oil
- 1 medium onion, quartered lengthwise and sliced ⅛ inch thick
- 1 celery rib, leaves removed, cut into sticks
- 1 large or 2 small kohlrabi, peeled and cut into slivers
- 1 carrot, peeled and slivered
- 3 tablespoons soy sauce
- Salt to taste

> If you substitute other vegetables for the ones called for here, aim for about 2 cups slivered vegetables.

Bring a large pot of water to a boil. Add pasta and cook for 7 to 8 minutes, or until barely tender. Drain in a colander.

Meanwhile, heat a large wok, heavy Dutch oven or wide iron skillet over high heat for 2 minutes. Add oil and swirl it around the pan to coat it.

Add onion, celery, kohlrabi and carrot to the pan and cook, stirring, for 2 minutes. Add pasta and stir rapidly over high heat, until vegetables are barely cooked, about 2 more minutes. Add soy sauce and a little salt and cook, stirring, for 1 minute more. Serve hot.

Serves 3. ~ Serve as a meal or pair with a side salad of sliced mushrooms or asparagus in Garlic Vinaigrette (page 15).

Summer Pasta Sauce

YOU COULD USE THIS SAUCE AS A SIDE DISH—it's rather ratatouille-ish—or as a sauce for omelets or rice. I like it with pasta. The eggplant will soak up the oil, so it's best to use a nonstick pan.

- 1 eggplant, 6-8 inches long
- 2 tablespoons olive oil or vegetable oil
- 3 large garlic cloves, minced, or more to taste
- 1 bell pepper (green, red or yellow)
- 1 28-ounce can tomatoes, with juice
- Salt and freshly ground pepper to taste
- ½ teaspoon crushed red pepper
- ½ cup imported black or green olives (optional)
- 8-12 ounces linguine or spaghetti
- ½ cup feta cheese or Parmesan, Asiago or another sharp cheese (optional)

One-half pound uncooked long pasta (a bunch about 1½ inches in diameter) yields about 4 cups cooked, enough for 4 average portions or 3 generous ones.

Peel eggplant, if desired, and cut into ½-inch cubes.

Heat oil in a Dutch oven or other deep, wide pot. Add eggplant and garlic and cook over medium heat as you cut bell pepper into ½-inch chunks. Add bell pepper to pan, increase the heat to medium-high, cover and cook for 5 minutes. Uncover and cook for 5 minutes more, stirring occasionally.

Increase the heat to high and add juice from canned tomatoes. Chop tomatoes into small pieces and add them to the pot. Bring to a boil, add salt (you'll need more salt if you plan to omit olives), pepper and crushed red pepper. Reduce the heat to medium-low to keep the mixture simmering briskly for about 15 minutes.

Rinse olives, if using, under hot running water, chop them into 2 or 3 pieces each and add them to sauce.

Meanwhile, bring a large pot of water to a boil, add salt, if desired, and pasta. Boil pasta for about 8 to 10 minutes, or until done to desired taste. Drain, toss with sauce and serve on plates or a platter and top with cheese, if using.

Serves 4. ~ Serve with rolls or Garlic (Cheese) Bread (page 196).

Asian Broccoli Noodles

YOU CAN ADD MORE NOODLES to this dish and it will serve more people, but I prefer the high proportion of broccoli.

If you like tofu, this recipe will readily accept ½ pound cut into ½-inch cubes. In that case, I increase the amount of noodles to 12 ounces to serve 6.

1 medium head broccoli
2 bunches green onions
1-2 large garlic cloves, minced
2 tablespoons peeled, minced fresh ginger
2 tablespoons peanut butter
¼ cup soy sauce
1 tablespoon sugar
3 tablespoons water or vegetable broth
Juice of 1 lemon (about 2 tablespoons)
½ teaspoon salt
8 ounces spaghetti or vermicelli
1-2 tablespoons vegetable oil

Trim and discard tough bottoms from broccoli. Cut florets into 1-inch pieces; peel stems, if using, and cut them into ½-inch squares.

Trim and discard roots and any wilted green tops from green onions. Mince green onions and combine in a small bowl with garlic, ginger, peanut butter, soy sauce and sugar. Stir to blend peanut butter, then add water or broth, lemon juice and salt.

Bring a large pot of water to a boil and cook noodles according to package directions, about 8 minutes for spaghetti, a little less for vermicelli, or until barely tender. Drain and rinse with cold water; drain again and set aside.

Heat a wok or other wide, deep cast-iron skillet over high heat for 3 or 4 minutes (if using an enameled or nonstick pan, don't heat without food in it). Add oil and broccoli. Stir-fry for 3 minutes. Add drained noodles, stirring constantly to heat them evenly.

Stir peanut butter mixture to distribute garlic and ginger, then add to the pan, stirring to distribute sauce evenly throughout. Serve hot.

Serves 2 to 4. ~ Serve with Ginger-Roasted Green Beans (page 156) or Roasted Honey-Mustard Carrots (page 153), sautéed spinach or sliced tomatoes.

Cauliflower with Long Noodles

My mother taught me to be deeply suspicious of fruit in main dishes. Raisins and nuts with cauliflower? C'mon!

But the combination was arrived at by Sicilians, who—stuck out there in the middle of the Mediterranean just a stone's throw from North Africa—learned a lot from the traders who passed through. Sweet raisins, salty olives, rich nuts on a plain vegetable: Make no mistake, this dish is delicious.

It tastes best if you use imported black olives, the kind packed in brine in jars, but you can substitute stuffed green olives. Don't expect to love this dish if you shake the cheese from a cardboard cylinder; buy a hunk of Parmesan to grate yourself or some feta to crumble.

- 1¼ pounds trimmed cauliflower florets or 4 heaping cups (from 2½ pounds untrimmed)
- 3 tablespoons olive oil
- 1 medium onion, chopped
- 2 large garlic cloves, minced
- ½ cup raisins
- ½ cup chopped pecans
- ½ cup sliced pitted imported black olives or stuffed green olives
- ¼ cup tomato paste (½ of a 6-ounce can)
- 12 ounces linguine
- ⅔ cup grated Parmesan or crumbled feta cheese

Bring a large pot of water to a boil.

Add cauliflower and cook for 3 minutes, or until tender. Scoop cauliflower out of the water using a slotted spoon. Save the water.

In a large pot, heat oil and sauté onion and garlic, stirring occasionally, until they are softened, about 3 to 5 minutes. Add raisins, nuts, olives, tomato paste and 1 cup cauliflower water. Simmer for 1 minute. Add cauliflower. Cover and simmer for 10 minutes.

Meanwhile, return cauliflower water to a boil and cook pasta for about 7 minutes, or until tender but still firm. Drain. Toss pasta with half of sauce and cheese. Top with remaining sauce and remaining cheese. Serve hot.

Serves 6. ~ Serve with Garlic (Cheese) Bread (page 196).

Greek-Style Noodles

THE BEST OF GREEK HOME COOKING is simple food that's easy to prepare. It depends on commonly available ingredients—high-quality fresh produce with loads of fresh parsley and oregano. Garlic is used less than you might think, while lemon is added liberally.

This dish is wonderful when it's made with curly noodles that are as long as spaghetti. Linguine is the next best choice, but any long noodle will work.

1 teaspoon salt
12 ounces linguine or spaghetti
5 tablespoons olive oil
1 cup minced fresh parsley
Grated zest and juice of 1 lemon
1 teaspoon dried oregano
Freshly ground pepper to taste
½ pound feta cheese

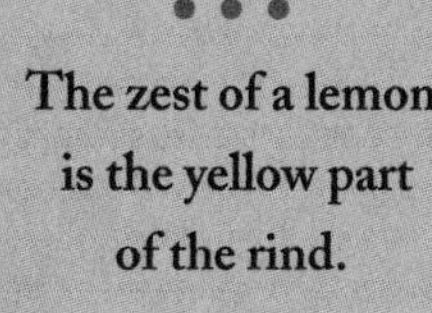

Bring a large pot of water to a boil and add salt. Cook noodles according to package directions, tasting them after they've cooked for half the time suggested on the package. The noodles are done when they are still very firm in the middle, about 6 minutes (they'll cook more later in the skillet).

Heat oil in a wide skillet. Add parsley, lemon zest and juice, oregano and pepper. Cook over medium heat to wilt parsley, 1 to 2 minutes, then lower the heat to keep ingredients warm.

Drain noodles but don't shake them dry. Put noodles in the skillet, crumble in half of feta and toss to coat noodles with herbs.

Serve noodles on individual plates or put them on a serving platter and crumble remaining cheese over top.

Serves 4 to 6. ~ Serve with Quick Greens and Red Bell Peppers (page 161) or broiled or sliced tomatoes, steamed asparagus or sautéed zucchini slices.

Greens and Noodles

GREENS AND NOODLES are fast and fabulous. This recipe calls for spinach or kale, but if other greens are more widely available, use them (many people prefer a mixture of kale and mustard greens). Some cooks make this with frozen spinach or even canned kale.

- 1 teaspoon salt, plus a little more
- 8 ounces small pasta shells, twists or bow ties
- 1 pound fresh spinach, kale or a mixture of greens
- 2 tablespoons olive oil
- 3 garlic cloves, minced
- ¼ teaspoon crushed red pepper
- Freshly ground pepper to taste
- ½ cup water or vegetable broth (optional)
- ½-1 cup freshly grated Parmesan or Romano, or Vermont or New York State Cheddar

• • •

The cheese makes this dish: Buy the best-quality aged cheese you can and grate it coarsely.

• • •

Bring a large pot of water to a boil and add salt. Add pasta and cook about 8 minutes, or until done to desired taste.

Wash and trim greens and slice into ribbons. Heat oil in a wide skillet, add garlic and cook for 2 to 3 minutes over medium heat, until it just begins to brown. Add greens by the handful, stirring and adding more when the first ones wilt. Add red pepper, salt and pepper. If you're using kale (or a mixture of tougher greens), you may want to add water or vegetable broth to slow the cooking and tenderize leaves.

When leaves are tender (about 5 minutes if you're using spinach, about 15 minutes if using tougher greens), toss with drained pasta and serve sprinkled with cheese.

Serves 4. ~ Serve with sliced mushrooms in Garlic Vinaigrette (page 15).

Pasta with Fresh Tomato Sauce

WHEN TOMATOES ARE IN SEASON—July through September in my area—I make pasta sauce with fresh tomatoes.

Some cooks have expressed dismay that sauce made with fresh tomatoes is "watery." I prefer to call it "juicy." Undercook the pasta so that it isn't quite al dente, then toss it with the juicy tomato sauce. The hot pasta will continue to cook and draw up the juice, making it more savory and eliminating much of the excess liquid.

1 teaspoon salt, plus a little more
12 ounces spaghetti, linguine or vermicelli
4 large tomatoes
2 tablespoons olive oil or vegetable oil
2 large or 4 medium garlic cloves, minced
2 teaspoons dried basil or ¼ cup minced fresh
Freshly ground pepper
2-4 tablespoons grated Parmesan or Asiago cheese

• • •

If you have access to fresh basil, use it.

• • •

Bring a large pot of water to a boil and add 1 teaspoon salt. When it boils, add pasta and cook for 8 to 10 minutes, or until done to desired taste.

At the same time, bring a small saucepan of water to a boil.

When it boils, add tomatoes, one at a time, and submerge for 10 seconds or turn tomato over halfway through cooking to submerge the other side. Remove tomato with a slotted spoon, set aside and repeat with remaining tomatoes. Core all tomatoes and remove their skins (skins should

just slip off). Cut them horizontally and use your finger to scoop out most of the seeds. Cut tomatoes in small chunks.

Heat oil in a wide skillet. Add garlic and cook over low heat for 2 to 3 minutes, being careful not to brown it. Add tomatoes, basil, salt and pepper to taste. Cook to heat through.

When pasta is cooked, drain, toss with sauce and half of cheese. Top with remaining cheese.

Serves 4. ~ Serve with plain green salad and rolls or Quick Fried Squash (page 162).

Quicker Tomato Sauce

WHEN TOMATOES AREN'T IN SEASON, use the canned crushed kind to make a delicious spaghetti sauce. This one is good with grilled or roasted vegetables chopped small and tossed with grated Parmesan or Asiago cheese.

You can double the recipe, but cook it in a Dutch oven so it doesn't spatter the stove. Any extra sauce can be frozen.

2 tablespoons olive oil
1 medium onion, chopped
2 garlic cloves, minced
1 teaspoon dried basil
1 teaspoon dried oregano
1 28-ounce can crushed tomatoes in puree
Salt and freshly ground pepper to taste

Heat oil in a wide skillet and add onion. Cook for 5 minutes, stirring, over medium heat, until softened.

Add garlic, basil and oregano. Cook for 2 to 3 minutes.

Pour in tomatoes, season with salt and pepper and simmer for 10 minutes, or until sauce reaches desired consistency.

If you don't have time to let the sauce reduce, add ½ can tomato paste and it will thicken instantly. You'll find recipes that use the other half-can elsewhere in this book.

(If you're using this mixture for spaghetti, let sauce simmer on low heat as you heat water and cook pasta.) Serve hot.

Serves 4. ~ Serve with plain green salad or a cooked green vegetable (beans, broccoli, asparagus, brussels sprouts), along with rolls.

Variation

Quick Tomato Sauce with Roasted Vegetables: Add 1 to 2 cups chopped Roasted Vegetable Mélange (page 165) to the sauce after it has cooked.

Beans

BEANS SHOW UP often in the world's poorest and healthiest cuisines. Unfortunately, that leaves Americans quite out of the picture, and until quite recently, beans have seemed intimidating or merely boring.

It's ironic, since they are easy, healthful and delicious. Relatively low in calories, they are high in complex carbohydrates and loaded with protein and the fiber that prevents heart attacks and cancer. They have vitamins and minerals to rival animal products, yet they are low on the food chain so that eating them keeps the earth healthy too.

To incorporate more beans in your menus, start with a dish that you love. Bean burritos with tons of sour cream and cheese are too fatty to eat often, but they might help you make the transition into bean burritos without so much fat or into other bean dinners.

My conversion dish was "Very Spicy Delicious Chick-Peas" from Madhur

Jaffrey's *World of the East Vegetarian Cooking* (Knopf, 1981)—a stew of beans simmered in a gravy rich with so many Indian seasonings that I was smitten. I lost my suspicion of these and subsequently of other beans. Now dinner at our house includes black beans and rice, black bean burritos, white beans and spaghetti, black-eyed peas and noodles, and red beans in chili.

Canned beans stand ready to become nearly instant dinners. They are the world's best convenience foods for budget-minded, time-constrained vegetarians. The possibilities are multiple:

- Open a can of black beans, stir in some chopped green chilies, sprinkle with a little Colby cheese and heat in the microwave.

- Heat pinto beans with a little salsa and chopped jalapeño pepper. Sprinkle with cheese and eat from a soup bowl, roll into tortillas or scoop up with tortilla chips.

- Combine white beans, cooked greens or broccoli with cooked spaghetti and top with Parmesan cheese.

- Combine red beans with minced red onion, cooked rice and a little vinaigrette seasoned with dill and garlic. Serve on top of lettuce leaves as a main-dish salad.

IT'S TRUE THAT THESE WONDER foods do cause gas as the bacteria in our intestines struggle to digest the beans' natural sugars. A little experimentation can solve this problem. Eat beans in small amounts—a few chick-peas in a minestrone, a few pinto beans in a taco salad—and see how they sit before you polish off three bowls of black bean chili. Cumin, ground coriander and ginger are all reputed to have beneficial effects on digestion. Beano, a commercial product sold through drugstores, can help reduce gas if you sprinkle a little on the beans before eating them.

If you take the time to cook your own beans, scientists advise boiling them in lots of water for 10 minutes, then soaking them overnight. Draining them and cooking them in two or three times their measure of water will likely cut down on most of those gas-causing sugars.

beans

Black Bean Chili

BLACK BEAN CHILI is a great Sunday afternoon project because it reheats well and can show up later during the week in another form. Not that it takes an entire day to prepare. If you add each ingredient to the pot as you prepare it, the dish can be made in as little as 30 minutes. Serve it in a bowl, then as a filling for Chilaquiles (page 124) or burritos (see page 180). Or freeze the extras.

If you're preparing it for company and don't want to add dairy products, scatter some minced red bell pepper and cilantro or parsley on the top to dress it up a little.

- 2 tablespoons vegetable oil
- 1 medium onion, diced
- 4 large garlic cloves, minced
- 4 teaspoons ground cumin
- 4 teaspoons dried oregano
- ½ teaspoon cayenne
- 1 4-ounce can chopped mild green chilies
- 3 16-ounce cans black beans (5-6 cups cooked)
- 1 15-to-16 ounce can diced or crushed tomatoes
- Salt and freshly ground pepper to taste
- Sour cream and/or Monterey Jack cheese (optional)

• • •

Minced fresh cilantro makes this chili taste even more fantastic.

• • •

Heat oil in a wide Dutch oven or other large pan over high heat. Add onions and garlic and cook, stirring occasionally to prevent burning. Add cumin, oregano, cayenne and green chilies.

When onions are soft, about 5 minutes, add black beans. Add tomatoes, salt and pepper. Bring to a boil, reduce the heat to low, and simmer mixture about 15 minutes, or until the flavors have blended. Serve topped with a little sour cream and/or grated cheese, if desired.

Serves 4. ~ Serve with tortilla chips and sliced oranges.

Rice with Limas

DRIED LIMA BEANS become creamier than other beans when they are cooked. Think of this dish as rice with bean gravy.

- 3 cups water
- 1 teaspoon salt, plus a little more
- 1½ cups long-grain white rice
- 3 tablespoons olive oil
- 1 small onion, sliced
- 2 large garlic cloves, minced
- 1 zucchini (5-7 inches long), sliced
- 1 teaspoon dried thyme leaves
- 2 16-ounce cans lima beans (4 cups cooked)
- Freshly ground pepper
- 1 medium tomato
- 1 cup grated provolone cheese or ¼ cup minced pitted black olives or stuffed green olives

To add extra flavor without using dairy products, top with minced imported black olives instead of the provolone cheese.

Bring water to a boil in a wide skillet, adding salt. Add rice, stir once, then cover and reduce the heat to low. Cook for about 18 minutes, or until water is absorbed and rice is tender.

Meanwhile, heat oil in another wide skillet or Dutch oven over high heat. Add onions, garlic, zucchini and thyme. Cook, stirring, until onions and zucchini are tender, about 5 to 10 minutes.

Add beans and cook until heated through, adding salt and lots of freshly ground pepper to taste. Halve tomato and scoop seeds out of the little seed pouches with your fingers. Chop tomato finely.

Serve beans over rice. Sprinkle with cheese or olives, then with tomatoes.

Serves 4 generously. ~ Serve with carrot sticks or red pepper strips, pear wedges or steamed asparagus.

Taco Salad with Red Beans

IF YOU'RE USING CHEESE on this salad, good choices include Monterey Jack, Cheddar or fontina. If your taste buds can handle it, try the Monterey Jack studded with jalapeño peppers.

- 1 4-ounce can chopped mild green chilies
- 1 teaspoon ground cumin
- 1 teaspoon chili powder
- 1 16-ounce can red beans in chili sauce
- 1 10-ounce package frozen corn (about 2 cups)
- 1 16-ounce can tomatoes, with juice
- Salt, freshly ground pepper and hot pepper sauce (optional) to taste
- 2-3 cups shredded lettuce
- ¼-½ pound cheese, grated (1-2 cups)
- 4 ounces low-fat or nonfat tortilla chips (about ½ of a 7-ounce bag or ⅓ of a 13½-ounce bag) or 4-6 crisped corn tortillas, broken

Combine green chilies, cumin, chili powder and beans in a wide skillet over medium heat. Add corn. Pour juice from canned tomatoes into the skillet, then remove tomatoes from the can one by one, and chop or squeeze them through your fingers so they break up as they fall into the skillet. Add salt, pepper and hot pepper sauce, if using. Simmer the mixture as you wash and shred lettuce, grate cheese and prepare the plates.

Divide tortilla chips or tortillas among 4 plates and top with equal amounts of lettuce and bean mixture, then sprinkle with cheese.

Serves 4 generously.

Black Beans and Rice

I LOVE THICK AND AROMATIC BEAN SAUCES over rice. Cumin, a classic spice for black beans, and mustard lend an interesting bite. You may want the dish spicier, so keep a bottle of hot sauce handy.

- 3 tablespoons olive oil
- 1 onion
- 1 red bell pepper
- 3 large garlic cloves
- 2 teaspoons ground cumin
- ½ teaspoon dry mustard
- 1 16-ounce can tomatoes, with juice
- 2 16-ounce cans black beans
- Salt, freshly ground pepper and hot pepper sauce to taste
- 1½ cups long-grain white rice

To give the dish a more Caribbean flavor, squeeze lime juice over the top just before serving.

Heat oil in a wide, deep pan over high heat. Mince onion and add it to oil. Mince red pepper, then garlic, adding them to the pot. Add cumin and mustard. Chop tomatoes in small pieces and add them along with their juice. Add black beans and seasonings as desired. Cook for 15 minutes or more to let flavors blend.

Meanwhile, cook rice: Bring 3 cups water to a boil, adding 1 teaspoon salt. Add rice, stir once, then cover and reduce the heat to low. Cook for about 18 minutes, or until water is absorbed and rice is tender.

Serve beans over rice.

Serves 6. ~ Serve with fresh raw vegetables or salad.

White Beans with Sage

THE COMBINATION of white beans and sage is a common one with an Italian heritage. It shows up in that country in many forms: in soups, stews and gratins. The result is earthy and completely satisfying, especially when served my favorite way—as a pasta sauce like this one.

3 tablespoons olive oil
1 onion, chopped
2-3 large garlic cloves, minced
2 16-ounce cans white beans (4 cups)
1 teaspoon salt
1 teaspoon freshly ground pepper
1 teaspoon dried sage leaves or 1 tablespoon fresh
¼ teaspoon crushed red pepper or cayenne
1 cup water or vegetable broth
½-¾ pound shell noodles or long noodles
½-1 cup grated Asiago or Parmesan cheese

If using dried sage, use leaf sage. Powdered sage doesn't have the right taste.

Heat oil in a wide skillet over high heat and add onion and garlic. Cook for 2 minutes, stirring. Onion will be barely tender. Add beans with their liquid, salt, pepper, sage, red pepper or cayenne and water or broth. Reduce the heat to low and simmer for about 10 minutes to blend flavors.

Bring a large pot of water to a boil. Add noodles and cook for about 10 minutes, or until done to desired taste. Drain well.

Taste beans and adjust seasonings. Put noodles in a large serving bowl and toss with 1 cup of beans. Pour remaining beans over the top and sprinkle with cheese.

Serves 4. ~ Serve with baked carrots in winter, fresh cherry tomatoes in summer.

Mediterranean Lentils and Rice

THIS RECIPE benefits from cinnamon and cumin. Though most of us associate cinnamon with desserts, other cultures add it to main dishes, combining it with savory spices, such as cumin, turmeric or pepper.

The saltiness of feta cheese goes well with the sweet spice mixture in the lentils.

- 2 tablespoons olive oil or vegetable oil
- 1 onion, minced
- 2 teaspoons ground cumin
- 1 teaspoon ground cinnamon
- ½ teaspoon cayenne, or to taste
- 1 teaspoon salt
- ¾ cup lentils
- 2 cups vegetable broth or water
- 1 14½-ounce can crushed tomatoes or diced tomatoes in puree
- ⅓ cup dried currants
- 2 cups water
- 1 cup long-grain white rice
- Crumbled feta or grated Parmesan cheese (optional)

• • •

If you can't get a 14½-ounce can of diced tomatoes, use a 15- or 16-ounce can, or buy whole tomatoes and chop them.

• • •

Heat oil in a wide skillet and add onions, cumin, cinnamon, cayenne and salt. Cook over medium-high heat until onions are soft, about 10 minutes (keep an eye on the heat—onions should cook fast but not burn).

Add lentils and broth or water and bring to a boil. Cover, reduce the heat to low and simmer for 30 minutes. Remove the cover and add tomatoes and currants. Bring to a boil, reduce the heat and cover again. Cook for 10 minutes more, or until lentils are tender.

Meanwhile, cook rice: Bring water to a boil, add rice, stir once, then cover and reduce the heat to low. Cook for about 18 minutes, or until water is absorbed and rice is tender.

Serve lentils over rice, topping with cheese, if desired.

Serves 4 to 6. ~ Serve with Quick Fried Cabbage (page 160) or Sweet Potato Medallions (page 155).

Ultra-Easy Lentils

IN THIS AND OTHER BEAN RECIPES, don't get hung up on precision. This recipe can be made with a 12- or 16-ounce package of lentils. I make mine with 16 ounces because that's the size available at my supermarket. The dish doesn't have a lot of broth, and I serve it on a plate over rice or couscous. If you make it with 12 ounces of lentils, it'll be soupier and you may want to stir the rice into it.

2 tablespoons vegetable oil
1 medium onion, minced
1 medium carrot, peeled and cut into small dice
3 large garlic cloves, minced
3 tablespoons peeled, minced fresh ginger
1 16-ounce package lentils (about 2 cups)
½ teaspoon salt, plus more to taste
Freshly ground pepper to taste
5 cups water or vegetable broth

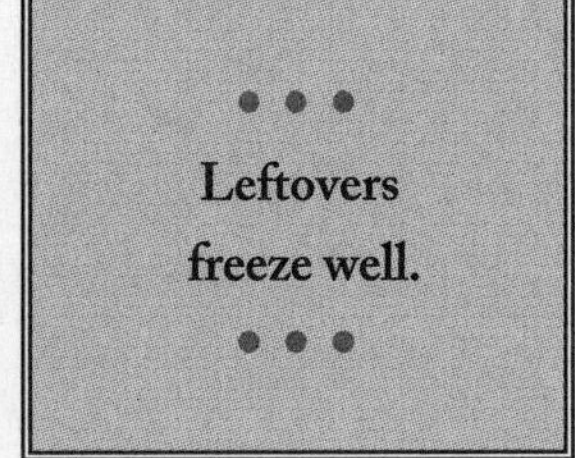
Leftovers freeze well.

Heat oil over medium heat and add onion, carrot, garlic and ginger. Cook until garlic and ginger are aromatic, 1 to 2 minutes.

Add lentils, salt, pepper and water or vegetable broth. Bring to a boil, then cover and reduce the heat to low. Cook for 40 minutes, or until lentils are tender. Season with salt and pepper.

Serves 6 generously. ~ Serve with or over rice (or couscous), with a side dish of sliced mangoes and muffins in the summer, baked acorn squash quarters in the winter.

Barbecued Black-Eyed Peas

THESE BEANS AREN'T REALLY BARBECUED. The sauce is barbecue-style—sweet, sour, spicy and aromatic all at once.

- 2 tablespoons vegetable oil
- 1 medium onion, chopped
- 1 carrot, peeled and chopped
- 1 celery rib (including leaves, if any), chopped
- 2 16-ounce cans black-eyed peas
- 1 6-ounce can tomato paste
- ¼ cup Worcestershire sauce
- 2 tablespoons apple cider vinegar
- 3 tablespoons light or dark brown sugar
- 2 teaspoons chili powder
- 1 teaspoon salt, or to taste
- 1 teaspoon freshly ground pepper, or to taste

Heat oil in a large skillet over medium-high heat. Add onion, carrot and celery as you prepare them, stirring occasionally.

When onions have softened, about 5 minutes, add remaining ingredients. Stir to blend, bring to a boil, then reduce the heat to low and simmer for 15 minutes to allow flavors to blend.

Serves 4. ~ Serve with Simple Corn Bread (page 198) and tossed salad or with potato salad and Sweet-and-Sour Cucumber Salad (page 27).

Lucky Beans and Rice

THIS ONE-POT MEAL uses frozen black-eyed peas, which are a little firmer and more separate than canned. The servings are large, but it's a delicious dish and so healthful that you want to eat a lot. I use diced tomatoes for this dish, but any comparable tomato product will work.

- 2 tablespoons vegetable oil or olive oil
- 4 garlic cloves, minced
- 1 green pepper, cored and diced
- 1 14½-ounce can diced tomatoes
- 1 10-ounce package frozen black-eyed peas
- ½ cup long-grain white rice
- ¾ cup water
- 1 teaspoon dried thyme leaves
- Salt and freshly ground pepper to taste
- ½ cup sharp Cheddar or jalapeño-studded Monterey Jack cheese

In a wide skillet, cook oil, garlic and green pepper over medium heat until softened, about 5 minutes.

Add tomatoes, black-eyed peas, rice, water, thyme and salt and pepper. Bring to a boil, cover and reduce the heat to low. Simmer for 18 minutes, or until rice is tender.

Serve topped with grated cheese.

Serves 4. ~ Serve with spinach or greens of choice sautéed with garlic and hot red pepper flakes.

White Beans and Greens

THE RECIPE CALLS FOR frozen leaf spinach instead of frozen chopped spinach because the dish is more appealing if there are large pieces of greens throughout rather than a more homogeneous look of pureed beans and greens. You can substitute fresh spinach for frozen, if you like. Clean, chop coarsely, then sauté in a little oil before adding the beans.

2 tablespoons olive oil
2 16-ounce cans white beans (3-4 cups cooked)
2 teaspoons vinegar (any kind)
½ teaspoon salt, or to taste
1 10-ounce package frozen leaf spinach, thawed and chopped
½ teaspoon crushed red pepper or cayenne, or to taste
1 cup grated Gruyère, extra-sharp Cheddar or freshly grated Parmesan cheese
1 cup unseasoned bread crumbs

> • • •
>
> Thaw frozen spinach in a microwave or over low heat in a small covered pan while you prepare the other ingredients.
>
> • • •

Preheat the oven to 425 degrees. Grease a gratin dish, an 8-by-8-inch baking pan or a similar-size dish with 1 tablespoon oil.

In a large bowl, combine beans and their liquid with remaining 1 tablespoon oil, vinegar and salt. Mash with a potato masher until mixture is a somewhat lumpy but thick puree.

Drain spinach and squeeze it dry, chop leaves and add to beans along with red pepper. Pour mixture into the greased dish and sprinkle with cheese and bread crumbs.

Bake for 20 minutes, or until bread crumbs are golden brown and mixture is bubbling.

Serves 4. ~ Serve with rice and sliced tomatoes, asparagus or Broccoli with Lemon-Caper Sauce (page 152) and Garlic (Cheese) Bread (page 196) or dinner rolls.

Chilaquiles

Chilaquiles is a Mexican version of that cheese-and-bread casserole so popular at American brunches—a sort of bread pudding with corn tortillas substituting for bread. It is the most comforting of comfort foods.

This dish is a great place to use stale tortillas, if you have any. Fresh ones work, though.

1 10-ounce package corn tortillas
2 tablespoons olive oil or vegetable oil
1 medium onion, chopped
1 4-ounce can chopped mild green chilies
½ jalapeño pepper, seeded and minced, or to taste
1 16-ounce can crushed tomatoes
1 16-ounce can pinto beans or black beans
½ pound Colby or Monterey Jack cheese
1 8-ounce container plain yogurt or 1 cup buttermilk

Preheat the oven to 375 degrees.

Heat tortillas briefly for 10 to 15 seconds directly on a gas flame or in a heavy, ungreased skillet on an electric stove. Use tongs to flip them constantly until they soften. Stack them and set aside.

Heat oil in a skillet and add onion. Cook over medium heat until soft, about 5 minutes. Add chilies, jalapeño and tomatoes and simmer.

In a separate bowl, coarsely mash beans, if desired. Grate cheese.

Butter a casserole dish (I use a 2-quart soufflé dish). Spoon some tomato-chili mixture into the casserole. Top with tortillas, cutting them to fit roughly in one layer (some will overlap; this is a free-form dish). Top with one-fourth of the beans, sprinkle with one-fourth of the cheese, then add a little more sauce. Add a layer of tortillas, then beans, cheese and sauce, making 3 more layers—or whatever your dish will hold. Spoon yogurt or pour buttermilk over top. Top with cheese. Cover tightly with foil and bake for 20 minutes. Remove the foil and cook for 20 minutes more, or until tortillas are soft and mixture is bubbling.

Serves 6. ~ Serve with a simple lettuce salad or sliced oranges sprinkled with cinnamon.

Spicy Chick-Peas

BUSY VEGETARIANS, like all busy cooks, need no-brainer meals, something they can put together quickly from familiar ingredients. This is one of those meals, with curry overtones and a tomato gravy. The cool yogurt and sweet-spicy chutney provide interesting contrasts to the soft and aromatic beans.

- 2 cups water
- ½ teaspoon salt, plus more to taste
- 1 cup long-grain white rice
- 2 16-ounce cans chick-peas (also called garbanzo beans), drained
- 1 28-ounce can crushed tomatoes
- 1-2 teaspoons curry powder
- ¼ teaspoon cayenne
- Freshly ground pepper to taste
- Plain low-fat yogurt
- Major Grey's or other brand chutney

• • •

This recipe is even more delicious with 1 to 2 teaspoons grated or chopped fresh ginger added with the other seasonings.

• • •

Bring water to a boil in a wide skillet, adding salt. Add rice, stir once, then cover and reduce the heat to low. Cook for 18 minutes, or until water is absorbed and rice is tender.

Meanwhile, in another wide saucepan or skillet, combine chick-peas, tomatoes, curry powder and cayenne. Bring to a boil, reduce the heat to low and simmer until heated through. Season with salt and pepper.

Serve over rice, topped with a spoonful of yogurt and chutney (if chutney is thick and chunky, you may want to chop it with a knife).

Serves 4. ~ Serve with green beans with Sesame Seed Sauce (page 143) or Roasted Vegetable Mélange (page 165).

Refried Beans with Garlic

REFRIED BEANS are supposed to be somewhat lumpy. You can roll them into flour burritos, dip into them with corn chips, top them with cheese, form them into patties and fry them and serve with rice or just scoop them up with a fork, as here.

1 tablespoon vegetable oil
2 medium garlic cloves, left whole
½ jalapeño pepper, minced (optional)
1 teaspoon ground cumin
½ teaspoon salt
½ teaspoon freshly ground pepper
2 16-ounce cans pinto beans (3-4 cups cooked)
1-2 cups grated Monterey Jack cheese (with or without jalapeño peppers)
Store-bought salsa
Chopped fresh cilantro (optional but delicious)
Warmed flour tortillas

Two 15- or 19-ounce cans of beans can also be used here. Chopped fresh tomatoes are also good with this.

Heat oil over medium heat in a wide skillet. Add garlic and jalapeño, if using, and cook, stirring occasionally, until garlic is browned all over. Add cumin, salt and pepper and stir to blend. Use a fork or the back of a wooden spoon to smash garlic to a chunky paste. Drain pinto beans and add. Mash them with a potato masher or beat with a handheld mixer to puree.

Spread bean mixture evenly in the skillet and top with cheese. When cheese melts, use a flat spatula to scoop out a serving, keeping the cheese side up. Serve with salsa and chopped fresh cilantro, if using, and tortillas. Let diners roll beans, salsa and cilantro into tortillas.

Serves 4. ~ Serve with a green salad and avocados with Garlic Vinaigrette (page 15).

Grains

When her oldest child unilaterally declared herself a vegetarian at the age of 8, my friend was dumfounded. What was left to have for dinner? For a long time, she struggled, serving regular family meals but omitting the meat from her daughter's plate.

Then she discovered bulgur. Whole wheatberries that have been precooked, dried and cracked, bulgur reconstitutes quickly in boiling liquid—sort of the whole-wheat version of Minute Rice. Bulgur's heritage is Middle Eastern, but my friend found it at her supermarket near the rice. She took it home, cooked it simply and served it with broccoli and acorn squash, founding the first of many vegetarian meals she would serve.

In health food sections and conventional grocery aisles, the average supermarket now holds a variety of grain-based products

that allow us to diversify our menus with foods that may have once been obscure, but that now fit right into American cuisine, piquing our interest without requiring long preparation.

Couscous is another good example. It looks like a grain, but it's really tiny beads of pasta. Like bulgur, it is found near the rice section and is precooked; it plumps up in boiling water in 5 minutes. It tastes like pasta, it couldn't be easier to fix and kids love it. Its nubbly texture is a fabulous foil for smooth and soft toppings, such as sweet potatoes, cooked squash and chick-peas.

OTHER TRADITIONAL American grains are being used in new ways. Grits, a traditional Southern breakfast, are no longer served just at breakfast anymore. They're more likely to be cooked in a casserole with cheese and/or chili like the one on page 137. Whole-kernel hominy, dried corn that has been treated with lye to remove the hulls, has a pleasantly musky tortilla flavor. Seasoned with cumin and chilies, it becomes a delicious dinner. Substituting canned hominy, which is found near the canned corn, for the traditional dried makes the dish much speedier (see page 138).

Pearled barley, located near the rice, is a nutty-tasting replacement for rice in pilafs and for noodles in casseroles. Although conventional barley takes 45 minutes to cook and is ideal for long-simmering soups and stews, the quick-cooking kind—found in most supermarkets—cooks in just 15 minutes, making the route to something different for dinner much more direct.

Grains

Bulgur Pilaf with Apricots and Sweet Potatoes

I KNOW WHAT YOU'RE THINKING: Sweet potatoes and apricots are just too darned weird for a pilaf or anything else. I thought so too. But the soft sweet potatoes play well between the nutty bulgur and the sweet-tart nuggets of apricots. Make it because it's great for your health; eat it because it tastes good. This recipe also is great with ¼ cup toasted chopped pecans stirred in.

- 3 tablespoons olive oil or butter
- 1 medium onion, finely chopped
- 1 pound sweet potatoes, peeled and cut into 1-inch squares
- 1 cup bulgur
- ¾ cup chopped dried apricots
- 2 cups water
- 1 tablespoon sugar
- Salt and hot pepper sauce to taste

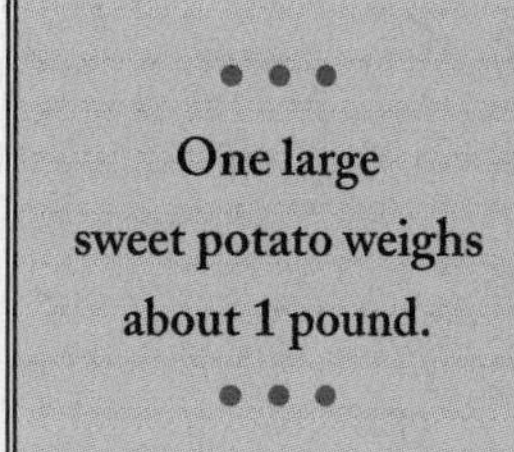

In a wide, deep skillet or Dutch oven, heat oil or melt butter. Add onions and sauté over medium heat, stirring frequently, until they begin to brown, 10 to 15 minutes.

Add sweet potatoes, bulgur, apricots, water, sugar, salt and hot pepper sauce. Cover, reduce the heat to low and simmer, stirring occasionally and adding more water, if necessary, until sweet potatoes are tender and bulgur is cooked through, about 15 minutes. Serve immediately.

Serves 6. ~ Serve hot, with bell peppers slivered and tossed with Garlic Vinaigrette (page 15) or Honey-Mustard Vinaigrette (page 16).

Bulgur and Dilled Zucchini

COMBINE CRACKED WHEATBERRIES (bulgur), fresh parsley and zucchini and you'll understand how good fast vegetarian food can be. This is a great meal for nights when you're distracted, because no precision is required. Does it matter whether the zucchini is in ¼-inch or ½-inch chunks? Heavens, no! Nor must you labor to get eensy leaves of parsley. But please do use fresh; it makes a big difference.

- 3 cups water
- 1 teaspoon salt
- 1½ cups bulgur
- 5 zucchini (5-7 inches long each)
- 2 tablespoons olive oil
- 1 cup chopped fresh parsley
- 1 tablespoon chopped fresh dill or 1 teaspoon dried
- ¼ teaspoon crushed red pepper (optional)
- About ½ cup crumbled feta cheese

> You'll find bulgur in the health food section of your supermarket or near the specialty rices.

Bring water to a boil in a medium pot and add salt. Add bulgur, cover, reduce the heat to low and cook for 5 minutes, or until barely softened. Remove from the heat; set aside.

Wash zucchini and cut into small cubes or slices about ¼ inch thick.

Heat oil in a wide skillet or wok over high heat. Add zucchini, parsley, dill and red pepper, if using. Cook until zucchini is done to desired taste, stirring frequently (I cook mine for about 10 minutes, until it is fairly tender).

If your pan is big enough, stir zucchini and bulgur together. If not, spoon bulgur onto plates and top with zucchini. Top with crumbled feta and serve.

Serves 4 to 6. ~ Serve with Sweet-and-Sour Cucumber Salad (page 27).

Variation

Zucchini with Tomatoes: Add a 16-ounce can stewed tomatoes or 3 fresh peeled tomatoes (chopped) to the skillet after the zucchini has cooked for about 5 minutes. Stir in or serve over bulgur.

Couscous with Eggplant Sauce

It may seem unusual to add allspice to main dishes, but it gives this vegetable stew an extra savory quality. I broil the eggplant to help it cook faster, while I work on the other parts of the dish. If you have a little extra time and would rather not wash an extra pan, dice the eggplant and add it to the skillet after cooking the onions, stirring occasionally over medium-high heat, until the eggplant is soft. (It can take up to 40 minutes to cook.)

1 large eggplant (1½ pounds)
1 medium onion
3 tablespoons olive oil
3 garlic cloves
¼ teaspoon ground allspice
Salt and freshly ground pepper to taste
1 28-ounce can diced tomatoes
¾ cup chopped walnuts and/or 1 cup roughly grated provolone, Gruyère or Cheddar cheese
3 cups water
2 cups couscous

> **You can substitute aromatic basmati rice for couscous, but omit the cheese.**

Heat the broiler. Peel eggplant, slice it lengthwise about ½ inch thick and place on a lightly oiled baking sheet. Broil for 5 minutes on each side, or until softened and slightly wrinkled.

Meanwhile, chop onion. Heat oil over medium heat in a wide, deep skillet and add onions. Cook for 5 minutes as you mince garlic. Add garlic, allspice, salt and pepper and tomatoes. Simmer briskly for another 5 minutes, until onions are soft.

Remove eggplant from the oven and dice it, adding it to the skillet. Simmer until thick, about 20 minutes.

Toast walnuts, if using, in a dry skillet over medium heat, stirring constantly, for 5 minutes, or until they are light brown and fragrant. Set aside.

Bring water to a boil in a wide skillet or pan. Add couscous and ½ teaspoon salt. Stir once, then cover and remove from the heat. Let stand for 5 minutes.

Spoon thickened eggplant sauce over couscous. Sprinkle with toasted walnuts and/or cheese.

Serves 4 to 6. ~ Serve with Quick Fried Cabbage (page 160), steamed broccoli or green beans.

Autumn Couscous

IF YOU CAN BOIL WATER, you can serve couscous for dinner. Here, it is topped with a cumin-scented Middle Eastern vegetable stew of chick-peas, sweet potatoes and tomatoes.

- **2 medium sweet potatoes**
- **2 tablespoons olive oil or vegetable oil**
- **3 large garlic cloves, minced, or more to taste**
- **1 teaspoon ground cumin**
- **½ teaspoon ground cinnamon**
- **2 green or red bell peppers, chopped**
- **1 28-ounce can tomatoes, chopped, with juice**
- **1 16-ounce can chick-peas (also called garbanzo beans)**
- **½ teaspoon crushed red pepper**
- **Salt and freshly ground pepper to taste**
- **3 cups water**
- **2 cups couscous**

> **You can substitute peeled, cubed winter squash or freshly cooked pumpkin for the sweet potatoes.**

Peel sweet potatoes and cut into ½-inch cubes. (You should have about 4 cups.)

Heat oil in a deep, wide pot. Add garlic, cumin, cinnamon and sweet potatoes and cook over medium heat, about 5 minutes. Add bell peppers, increase the heat to medium-high, cover and cook for 5 minutes. Uncover and cook for 5 minutes more, stirring occasionally. Increase the heat to high; add tomatoes and juice. Bring to a boil and add chick-peas, red pepper, salt and pepper. Reduce the heat to low and simmer for about 15 minutes, until sweet potatoes are tender.

Boil the water in a small pot with ½ teaspoon salt. Add couscous, cover and remove from the heat. Set aside for 5 minutes. Fluff with a fork; spoon sweet-potato sauce over couscous and serve.

Serves 4 to 6. ~ Serve with rolls or Garlic (Cheese) Bread (page 196).

Cheese Grits

When cooked plain, grits taste somewhat like corn and go well with cheese. (They are found near the oatmeal in the supermarket.) The following dish, bolstered with a heady amount of garlic, has been appreciated by the bluest-blooded Bostonians as well as Southerners.

4 cups water
1 teaspoon salt
1 cup quick grits
¼ cup (½ stick) butter
2 garlic cloves, minced
1 cup grated Cheddar or other sharp cheese
Hot sauce to taste
Paprika and/or ground cayenne (optional)

Serve these straight from the pan or, for convenience and a firmer result, bake in a casserole dish.

If you plan to bake grits, preheat the oven to 350 degrees and butter a 2-quart casserole dish.

Bring water and salt to a boil in a large, heavy pot over high heat. Add grits in a steady stream, beating constantly to prevent lumps. When mixture boils again (it may never stop), reduce the heat to low and, stirring occasionally, cook until grits are quite thick, 4 to 5 minutes.

Meanwhile, melt butter in a small saucepan. Add garlic and cook over medium-high heat for 1 to 2 minutes, until it is aromatic.

Remove grits from the heat, stir in garlic-butter mixture, cheese and a little hot sauce. Stir to blend. Serve from the pot, sprinkled with paprika and/or cayenne, or pour into the casserole, sprinkle with paprika and/or cayenne and bake for 30 minutes, or until bubbly.

If you'd like to make grits ahead, fill the casserole, cool slightly, cover and refrigerate. Heat in a 350-degree oven for 45 minutes, or until heated through.

Serves 6. ~ Serve with greens and applesauce or with green beans and Broiled Tomatoes (page 164) or tomato slices.

Green Chili Hominy

In the South and Southwest, dried hominy is often simmered for hours with pork and green chilies. I prepare a speedy vegetarian version made with canned hominy, cheese and spices.

- 2 tablespoons vegetable oil or olive oil
- 3 garlic cloves, minced
- 1 medium onion, chopped
- 1 teaspoon ground cumin
- ½ teaspoon ground coriander
- 1 29-ounce can hominy
- 1 4-ounce can chopped mild green chilies
- Salt and freshly ground pepper or crushed red pepper to taste
- Minced green onions and/or grated Cheddar or Monterey Jack cheese (optional)

> Canned hominy is usually found near the canned corn at the supermarket.

Heat oil in a wide skillet over medium heat and add garlic, onions, cumin and coriander. Cook, stirring occasionally, over medium heat, until onions are soft, about 10 minutes.

Add hominy and chilies and cook to heat through and evaporate liquid. Taste and season with salt, pepper and red pepper, if desired. Sprinkle with green onions and/or grated cheese, if using.

Serves 3 to 4. ~ Serve with sliced tomatoes and Quick Fried Squash (page 162) in the summer, Quick Fried Cabbage (page 160) in the winter.

Barley-Mushroom Pilaf

PILAF IS A MIXTURE of starch (usually rice) and vegetables seasoned with herbs and sometimes bits of meat. I've replaced the rice with nutty, chewy barley and added walnuts for a rich, meaty flavor.

- 2 cups water
- 1 cup quick-cooking barley
- ½ pound fresh mushrooms
- 2 tablespoons olive oil
- 3 garlic cloves, minced
- ¼ cup chopped walnuts or pine nuts
- 1 10-ounce package frozen spinach, thawed and squeezed dry
- 2 teaspoons dried dill
- 1 teaspoon salt
- ½-1 teaspoon freshly ground pepper
- 1 cup grated cheese (Parmesan, Gruyère, Cheddar)

Bring water to a boil in a medium saucepan. Add barley, stir once, reduce the heat to low and simmer until tender, about 10 minutes.

Meanwhile, wash mushrooms and shake or pat dry. Heat oil in a wide skillet. Add garlic and nuts and cook over medium heat as you slice mushrooms thinly.

When nuts are toasted, add mushrooms and spinach, increasing the heat to high. Add dill, salt and pepper and stir. Cook until mushrooms are softened and somewhat shrunken, 10 to 15 minutes. Mix with barley, then toss lightly with cheese, saving a little to sprinkle on top.

Serves 4 to 6. ~ Serve with Broiled Tomatoes (page 164) or Quick Fried Squash (page 162).

Vegetables

Being a vegetarian doesn't guarantee you have lots of extra time. We're no less busy than omnivores, but we look at vegetables in a new way—as major dietary players. We could go on eating the steamed carrots that used to accompany our chicken breast, but roasting them is not only easier than steaming, it's better. And then you catch yourself saying, "Hey, these carrots taste really good!" Then you wonder, will they taste just as fabulous stir-fried in a wok with garlic and soy sauce? And maybe the spinach would also taste good with soy sauce and garlic, perhaps with a few sesame seeds thrown in. Pretty soon, you have a week's worth of delicious vegetable dishes that, along with a big mound of rice or some noodles, make a great dinner.

Whatever vegetables I serve, I want them to taste so good that I can plan a meal around them, like Green Bean Stew, a traditional Greek specialty that is super-easy (see page 150). They need to be ready in an

instant, like Quick Fried Cabbage (page 160). And for those most time-challenged moments, I need a foolproof main dish, like Mixed Vegetable Stir-Fry (page 146).

Try these suggestions for getting your vegetables to the table better and faster:

● Consider using your supermarket's salad bar. The best bargains are the lightweight items that require lots of labor to prepare. Fresh spinach is first on the list—it's already washed and ready for a quick sauté. Look for cabbage to make quick slaw, mushrooms to dress with vinaigrette.

● Perfect a few good toppings. Sprinkle steamed or sautéed vegetables with a little grated cheese. On rushed nights, sauté broccoli, green beans or cauliflower with garlic and olive oil and sprinkle it with Romano or Parmesan, crumbly aged Cheddar, a little blue cheese or feta.

● A drizzle of olive oil seasoned with garlic, melted butter studded with capers, or soy sauce and sesame seeds make a plate of plain steamed vegetables into a real meal.

● Choose the best frozen vegetables. I stay away from mixtures with pasta, rice and butter coatings, which add a lot to the cost. Even *I* can melt butter! But mixing florets of broccoli and cauliflower with pieces of carrot takes time and requires lugging a bunch of stuff home from the store. A frozen mixture of the three is lightweight, nutritious and makes great fried rice.

● Choose fresh, seasonal vegetables when you can. They're usually tastier and cheaper. You'll find bargains and good eating if you buy zucchini and eggplant in summer, spinach and lettuce in the fall and spring, sweet potatoes and butternut squash in autumn, root vegetables in winter.

● Serve raw vegetables as a side dish, not just in salad. Cut up red and green peppers, radishes, carrots, celery, broccoli and/or cauliflower and pass them at the table, perhaps with homemade dip or bottled dressing.

vegetables

Sesame Seed Sauce for Vegetables

SERVE THIS ON THE SIDE or on top of cooked vegetables, such as broccoli, cabbage, winter squash, sweet potatoes or zucchini. I especially like it with green vegetables: broccoli, green beans and sautéed fresh spinach.

¼ cup sesame seeds
2 teaspoons sugar
2 tablespoons vinegar (any kind)
3 tablespoons soy sauce

Toast sesame seeds in a dry heavy skillet over medium heat. Stir them frequently, removing the pan from the heat for several seconds if they seem to be cooking unevenly. When they are golden and smell toasty, remove from the heat.

Combine sugar, vinegar and soy sauce in a jar or dish. Stir to dissolve sugar and stir in sesame seeds.

Makes about ⅓ cup.

Adding dark amber, nutty-smelling Asian sesame oil will make this sauce even more delicious. Just a teaspoon will make a dramatic difference.

Asparagus with Brown Butter and Capers

VEGETABLES OFTEN BENEFIT from a tart component, as evidenced by the use of such sauces as lemon juice or hollandaise. Here, capers give an aromatic sprightliness to a garlic-butter sauce. Perfect asparagus will look relatively fresh at the cut end, still have some white attached and have compact buds at the top. But it doesn't have to be perfect to be great in this recipe.

1 pound asparagus
2 tablespoons butter
2 garlic cloves, left whole
2 tablespoons capers

Wash asparagus and cut away and discard any woody stems.

Melt butter in a wide skillet. Add garlic cloves and capers and cook over medium-high heat until butter and garlic begin to brown, about 3 minutes.

Meanwhile, cut asparagus into 2-inch lengths. Add asparagus to the skillet and stir. Cook, stirring often, until asparagus is bright green and tender, 1 minute for very thin asparagus, 4 to 5 for thicker spears. Remove and discard garlic before serving.

Serves 4. ~ Serve hot with rice or as part of a vegetable plate that includes other spring vegetables, such as lettuce and peas.

Mediterranean Stir-Fry

THESE FRESH, crisply cooked vegetables tossed with olive oil and garlic taste great with noodles, over rice or served by themselves. Like all stir-fries, this Mediterranean one goes faster if you prepare the ingredients ahead of time.

1 green or red bell pepper
¼ pound fresh mushrooms
2 zucchini (5-7 inches long each)
1 small onion
1 large garlic clove
1 tablespoon olive oil
1 teaspoon dried oregano
1 cup grated Parmesan or provolone cheese (optional)

Wash, core and slice bell pepper into thin strips. Clean and slice mushrooms. Wash zucchini, trim ends and slice about ¼ inch thick. Slice onion. Mince garlic.

Heat oil in a wide skillet or Dutch oven over high heat. Add onion and cook, stirring, for 1 minute. Add garlic and bell pepper and cook, stirring, for 2 minutes. Add mushrooms, zucchini and oregano and cook to desired texture, stirring occasionally. (I cook mine for about 5 minutes.)

Sprinkle with grated cheese, if using.

Serves 4 as a side dish, 2 as a main dish over rice or noodles.

Mixed Vegetable Stir-Fry

THIS RECIPE can be made with either fresh or frozen vegetables. When I'm in a hurry, I choose bags of frozen mixed cauliflower, broccoli and carrots (you'll need 3 to 4 cups) and add my own fresh cabbage. Virtually any kind works: napa, savoy, bok choy or regular green cabbage.

Sauce

2 cups vegetable broth
2 tablespoons soy sauce
1½ tablespoons cornstarch

Vegetables

2 tablespoons vegetable oil
1 tablespoon peeled, minced fresh ginger
1-3 teaspoons minced garlic
2 carrots, peeled and sliced diagonally ¼ inch thick
1–2 cups cauliflower florets, cut small
3 cups sliced cabbage (savoy, Chinese or regular green)
Soy sauce
Hot pepper sauce
½-¾ cup chopped toasted cashews

• • •

If you want to serve this dish over rice, start the rice before you prepare the vegetables. If you can get Asian ingredients, try this with a dollop of chili paste.

• • •

To make sauce: Combine broth, soy sauce and cornstarch in a bowl. Set aside.

To make vegetables: Heat a wok or large cast-iron skillet over high heat for 3 minutes (if your skillet is nonstick or coated with enamel, heat it for only a few seconds). Add oil, then add ginger and garlic. Add carrots and cauliflower and stir-fry for about 1 minute. Add sliced cabbage and stir-fry for 30 seconds.

Stir the sauce to completely blend cornstarch, then pour into the skillet. Stir to coat. Cook, stirring, until sauce is thick and clear, about 1 minute. Add soy sauce and hot pepper sauce to taste. Serve hot, topped with cashews.

Serves 4. ~ **Serve with hot rice.**

Farmer's Garden Stir-Fry

In the Far East, peanuts are commonly used to add intense flavor to vegetables and noodles. These will look like big helpings, but your family will probably be able to eat the whole dish in one sitting. You can use any leftovers in fried rice, adding fresh ginger and garlic to the vegetables.

3 cups water
1 teaspoon salt
1½ cups long-grain white rice

Sauce

1 bunch green onions
½ cup soy sauce
2 tablespoons peanut butter
1 tablespoon vinegar (any kind)
1 teaspoon sugar
½ teaspoon crushed red pepper

Vegetables

2 tablespoons vegetable oil
2 cups fresh green beans, cut on the diagonal, or frozen beans
1 small yellow squash, sliced ½ inch thick
1 small zucchini, sliced ½ inch thick
1 green bell pepper, sliced

• • •

The best soy sauce is the kind that's naturally fermented. Kikkoman, commonly found in supermarkets, is a good example, but there are others.

• • •

Bring water to a boil in a large pot, adding salt. Add rice, stir once, then cover and reduce the heat to low. Cook for about 18 minutes, or until water is absorbed and rice is tender.

To make sauce: Trim and discard roots and any wilted green tops from green onions. Chop green onions and combine in a small bowl with soy sauce, peanut butter, vinegar, sugar and red pepper. Stir to blend liquid with peanut butter. Set aside.

To make vegetables: Heat oil in a large skillet, Dutch oven or wok. When it is quite hot, add green beans and stir-fry for 3 minutes for fresh, 2 minutes for frozen. Add yellow squash, zucchini and green peppers and stir-fry for another 2 minutes.

Add sauce and cook, stirring, until vegetables are coated and heated through, or until they reach the texture you like.

Serves 3 or 4 over rice.

Green Bean Stew

GREEN BEAN STEW is a standard selection at every Greek festival and on every Greek menu I've ever seen. That's because it's easy and delicious and tastes great reheated.

You can put a lot of effort into this dish by using fresh ingredients. But you can also take shortcuts with canned tomatoes and frozen green beans, especially in winter.

¼ cup olive oil
3 medium onions, chopped
½ jalapeño pepper, minced, or ½ teaspoon crushed red pepper or cayenne
1½ pounds fresh green beans or three 10-ounce packages frozen
½ cup water
2 teaspoons dried dill
1 teaspoon salt
Freshly ground pepper to taste
3 cups peeled, cored fresh tomatoes or one 28-ounce can crushed tomatoes
1 cup crumbled feta cheese (optional)

One and a half pounds of fresh, cut-up green beans makes 5 to 6 cups.

Heat oil in a Dutch oven or other wide, deep pan over high heat. Add onions and jalapeño or other hot pepper. Add green beans, water, dill, salt and pepper. Cook for 10 minutes, or until beans are barely tender.

Add tomatoes, stir and cook for 5 to 10 minutes more, or until green beans are cooked enough to suit you. Serve topped with crumbled feta cheese, if desired.

Serves 4 as a main dish, 6 to 8 as a side dish. ~ Serve hot with rolls and corn on the cob in summer, baked potatoes in winter.

Eggplant "Pizza"

THIS RECIPE IS A LITTLE TROUBLE, but it's delicious and light. It's reminiscent of eggplant Parmesan without the frying. And it cooks faster because the eggplant is in one layer. Save more time by using ready-made tomato sauce, such as spaghetti or pizza sauce.

2 eggplants (6-8 inches long each), peeled and cut into ½-inch-thick slices
About 2 tablespoons olive oil or vegetable oil
1 8-ounce can tomato sauce
2 large garlic cloves, minced
1 teaspoon dried basil
½ teaspoon dried oregano
Up to ½ cup cottage cheese (optional)
1-2 cups grated provolone, mozzarella or Swiss cheese

To peel garlic quickly, press down firmly with the flat side of a knife. The skin will pop away from the garlic.

Preheat the broiler. Brush a wide, shallow baking sheet with oil.

Place eggplant rounds in a single layer on the baking sheet and brush them with oil. You may have to cook them in batches. Broil about 4 inches from the heat for about 5 minutes on each side, or until browned and tender. Remove from the oven; set aside. Reduce the heat to 450 degrees.

While eggplant cooks, mix tomato sauce, garlic, basil and oregano in a small bowl, stirring to mix evenly.

Spread each eggplant round with tomato sauce, place a teaspoon or two of cottage cheese on top of each, if desired, and sprinkle with cheese. Bake for 5 minutes, or until cheese melts, and serve.

Serves 6. ~ Serve with noodles, peas and Garlic (Cheese) Bread (page 196). Leftovers microwave well and also make a great sandwich filling on sturdy whole-grain bread, poppy-seed or sesame buns or French bread.

Broccoli with Lemon-Caper Sauce

Broccoli is one of my family's favorite vegetables, and we never tire of finding new ways to fix it. My children prefer a flour-thickened cheese sauce to all others, but it takes a little work. This sauce is no bother at all and it's fabulous. For a more substantial dish, toss the broccoli with curly egg noodles and top with Parmesan cheese.

You'll find capers in your supermarket near the pickles and olives. The smallest ones are the most expensive. To save money, you can buy the bigger ones (none are very big) and chop them.

1½ pounds broccoli
2 tablespoons olive oil
1 tablespoon vinegar or juice of ½ lemon
1 tablespoon capers (or substitute 1 tablespoon minced green olives)
Dash cayenne

Fill a large pot with 3 to 4 inches of water. Cover and bring to a boil. Trim broccoli to make florets, peel stems, if using, and cut stems into ½-inch pieces. When water boils vigorously, add broccoli all at once. Cook for 5 minutes, or until bright green and barely tender.

Mix remaining ingredients. Drain broccoli, drizzle with caper sauce and serve immediately.

Serves 4. ~ Serve with Warm Potato Salad (page 83).

Tender-cook the broccoli any way you prefer. I like boiling it in water, but if you've mastered the microwave or the steamer, that's okay too.

Roasted Honey-Mustard Carrots

CARROTS ARE GOOD FOR YOU, inexpensive, always available and keep well in the refrigerator—so much the better that they are universally loved. A good carrot recipe is your ace in the hole for any meal, and roasting brings out the best in them. Roast them plain, if you like, or with a tangy honey-mustard sauce.

1 pound carrots
1 tablespoon olive oil or vegetable oil
2 tablespoons honey
2 tablespoons water
1 tablespoon vinegar (any kind)
1 tablespoon Dijon-style mustard
½ teaspoon salt
½ teaspoon freshly ground pepper

Preheat the oven to 400 degrees. Brush a wide, shallow baking sheet with oil.

Peel carrots and cut them into sticks about 3 inches by 2 inches. Place on the baking sheet and roast for 10 minutes.

Meanwhile, stir together honey, water, vinegar, mustard, salt and pepper. Remove carrots from the oven and stir mustard sauce into them. Roast for 10 minutes more, or until carrots are tender.

Serves 4 to 6. ~ Serve with baked potatoes and mushrooms sautéed with garlic.

Quick Cauliflower Curry

IF BEAUTY IS AS BEAUTY DOES, cauliflower is Ms. Universe. Full of cancer-fighting substances, it is also low in calories and high in fiber. And it's beautiful to look at too.

2 tablespoons olive oil or vegetable oil
1 garlic clove, minced
1 teaspoon ground ginger
1 teaspoon salt
1 teaspoon ground cumin
½ teaspoon ground turmeric
1 head cauliflower, trimmed and cut into florets
¼ cup water

Heat oil in a wide skillet. Add garlic, ginger, salt, cumin and turmeric. Cook briefly, stirring. Add cauliflower and water, cover tightly, reduce the heat to low and simmer until cauliflower is tender, about 10 minutes. Serve immediately.

Serves 4 to 6. ~ Serve with baked potatoes and peas or serve it over or stirred into cooked rice, with carrots alongside.

This blend of spices produces a curry mixture that can be added to other foods, including tomatoes, potatoes and summer squash.

Sweet Potato Medallions

SWEET POTATOES require long, slow baking to develop their full sweetness, but when you cut them into slices, you decrease the amount of time they need to bake. I love the combination of honey and black pepper in this recipe. Try it with winter squashes, such as acorn, butternut or buttercup.

3 large sweet potatoes, sliced about 1 inch thick
Olive oil or vegetable oil
2-3 teaspoons honey
Salt and freshly ground pepper to taste

> You can cook white potatoes this way, but omit the honey.

Preheat the oven to 450 degrees.

Peel sweet potatoes only if you want to. Slice them into disks about 1 inch thick. Grease a wide baking sheet (I use my darkest one so the medallions brown better) with a generous amount of oil. Place sweet potato slices on the baking sheet, then turn them to coat both sides with oil. Dab a tiny bit of honey on all slices, then sprinkle with salt and pepper.

Bake for 20 minutes, or until the slices are nicely browned on the bottom and tender. Serve hot.

Serves 4 to 6. ~ Serve sprinkled with feta cheese, if desired, as a main dish with sliced kiwifruit and plain bulgur.

Ginger-Roasted Green Beans

I cook with another family every Thursday night. My friend makes the kids' dinner and I do the grown-ups' meal. It works beautifully, everyone gets along and, what the heck—they do the dishes. But the dad in this family cannot tolerate onions. So when I cook with them, I rely a lot on fresh ginger, which makes ordinary food taste exotic.

- **1 pound fresh green beans**
- **2 tablespoons vegetable oil**
- **4 large garlic cloves**
- **1 tablespoon peeled, grated fresh ginger**
- **½ jalapeño pepper, seeded and minced, or ½ teaspoon crushed red pepper, or to taste**
- **1 tablespoon water**
- **1 tablespoon soy sauce**
- **1 teaspoon sugar**
- **2 green onions, trimmed and chopped (optional)**

Large garlic cloves will cook at the same rate as the beans. If you use small ones, keep your eye on them and remove them if they begin to turn dark brown.

Preheat the oven to 425 degrees.

Trim beans and break them into shorter lengths, if desired. Spread them on a wide, shallow baking pan. Drizzle with oil and toss to coat. Peel garlic and toss with beans. Bake for 20 minutes, stirring twice during cooking and removing any garlic that's turning deep brown, until beans shrivel and are tender.

Meanwhile, combine ginger, jalapeño or red pepper, water, soy sauce and sugar. Stir to blend.

Remove beans from oven and toss with soy-sauce mixture. Serve hot, warm or cold on plates or a platter, sprinkled with green onions.

Serves 4. ~ Serve with plain white rice and fried apples, or as part of a vegetable plate or with a plain baked potato and cherry tomatoes vinaigrette.

Kale and Currants

I LEARNED TO LOVE KALE prepared this way, and it's one of my favorite recipes. Plain kale had never tempted me. But the pine nuts and currants sounded promising, not to mention the garlic and feta cheese. I wasn't disappointed.

This chewy, coarse vegetable is great for people who would love to eat more cooked greens but remember only the slimy cooked spinach of their youth. Kale doesn't get slimy.

Be flexible with the proportions here—12 cups, 15 cups, 10 cups of kale—having an exact amount doesn't matter. If it seems a little too chewy, add water and simmer it for a little longer. There shouldn't be much extra liquid when you serve it, though.

2 tablespoon dried currants
½ cup hot water
2-3 tablespoons chopped pine nuts or pecans
3 bunches kale
2-3 tablespoons olive oil
3 garlic cloves, finely chopped
Salt and freshly ground pepper to taste
¼ cup crumbled feta cheese

If you don't have currants, chop dark or golden raisins. You don't want any powerhouses of sweet bursting in your mouth; you want little bits hidden throughout the dish.

Preheat the oven to 350 degrees.

Combine currants with ¼ cup hot water and set aside. Toast nuts in the oven until fragrant, about 10 minutes, but keep an eye on them. Pine nuts toast faster than pecans.

Wash kale well, trim tough stem ends and shake off any excess moisture. Gather leaves in a bunch and use a sharp knife to cut them into ribbons about 1 inch wide. You should have about 12 cups.

Heat oil in a wide skillet. Add garlic and cook over medium heat for about 2 minutes. Add kale and use tongs or a couple of spoons to toss. Greens will be heaping at first, but they wilt quickly. Sprinkle with salt and pepper, add remaining ¼ cup water and cover. Cook over medium heat until leaves are as tender as you like them, about 10 to 15 minutes.

Add currants and their soaking liquid and cook, tossing to evaporate most of liquid. Add more salt and pepper, if necessary. Remove to individual plates or a platter, sprinkle with nuts and feta cheese and serve.

Serves 4 to 6. ~ Serve with baked potatoes and sliced tomatoes or with spaghetti and sautéed red pepper strips.

Quick Fried Cabbage

CABBAGE IS PART of that cruciferous gang that keeps cancer at bay, and it's also high in vitamin C, which this quick-cooking recipe keeps intact. You can use any kind for this dish, but the timing specified here is for conventional green-head cabbage. If you choose leafier savoy or one of the Chinese cabbages, reduce the cooking time to keep it nearly raw and fresh-tasting.

½ head cabbage
2 tablespoons olive oil
Salt and pepper to taste

Cut cabbage in half again vertically through the core. Then cut each piece in half. Save 2 quarters for another use. Cut the cores out of the other 2 pieces, then cut across each one at 2-inch intervals.

Heat oil in a wide skillet over high heat. Add cabbage, sprinkle with salt and pepper and cook, stirring, for 3 to 5 minutes, until cabbage is hot and glossy but still crunchy.

Serves 4 to 6. ~ Serve with sweet potatoes and ripe pears or baked potatoes and baked zucchini.

Choose this dish when you need an ultra-quick side dish for starchy main dishes.

Quick Greens and Red Bell Peppers

I PREFER KALE, but other greens will work fine here. Southern cooks often cook mixtures of greens: mustard and chard, turnip and kale. This dish is prettiest with red bell pepper but will taste good with green, yellow, purple or any other color you have. Because greens are high in calcium, they are especially important if you avoid dairy products.

- 1 tablespoon vegetable oil
- 1 onion (red is good), cut in half and sliced thinly
- 1 large red bell pepper
- ½ jalapeño pepper or ½ teaspoon red pepper flakes, or to taste
- 3 tablespoons water
- 2 tablespoons soy sauce
- Salt to taste
- 1 pound greens of choice, washed and slivered (4-6 cups)

> One-half teaspoon crushed red pepper makes a spicy dish. Adjust as you see fit.

Heat oil in a wok or Dutch oven over high heat. Add onion and stir-fry for about 2 minutes; it should still be crisp. Add red bell pepper and jalapeño, if using, and stir-fry for 2 minutes more. If using red pepper flakes instead of jalapeño, add now along with water, soy sauce, salt and greens.

Toss a few times, then cover, reduce the heat to medium-high and cook until done to desired taste, 5 minutes or more, adding water as necessary. The final dish should have a little juice, but not much.

Serves 4. ~ **Serve with corn bread and pinto beans or with rice and sliced tomatoes.**

Quick Fried Squash

I OFTEN HAVE MOMENTS of dinner-planning anxiety when I've nailed down what the main dish will be but am still wondering what the heck I can serve with it. This savory squash, cooked in olive oil and sprinkled with cheese, is a stalwart in my instant-side-dish file. Mild peppers (such as bell peppers or Italian peppers) can be prepared the same way.

If the squashes are longer than 7 inches, don't use them. Large squashes are woody, tough and watery-tasting.

4-5 small (4-5 inches long) yellow squash, zucchini or other summer squashes
2 tablespoons olive oil
Salt and lots of freshly ground pepper
1-2 teaspoons grated Parmesan cheese or capers

Wash squashes, trim ends and cut them in half lengthwise. If they are longer than 4 inches, you may want to cut them into 3 lengthwise slices.

Heat oil in a wide skillet over medium-high heat. Add squashes, cut sides down, and cook until deep brown, about 10 minutes. Turn them over and cook until squashes are softened all the way through (the yellow side won't get so brown). Sprinkle with salt and pepper to taste, place on a platter or plates and sprinkle with cheese or a few capers with their pickling juice.

Serves 4. ~ Serve with pasta dishes or any main dish.

Baked Zucchini

In the height of summer, there's usually more zucchini than we know how to use. Our gardens our full, the arms of our neighbors are full, the produce bins at the supermarket are full of zucchini at tempting prices. This is a dish for that season. Bread crumbs and cheese play off the creamy zucchini. Think of it as a casserole, only simpler. You can assemble it ahead of time and finish baking it at your convenience.

4 zucchini (5-7 inches long each)
2 tablespoons olive oil or vegetable oil
2-3 garlic cloves, minced
½-1 cup grated cheese (Parmesan, Asiago, Romano)
½-1 cup unseasoned dry bread crumbs

Choose zucchini no longer than 7 inches—they make the best eating.

Preheat the oven to 400 degrees. Wash zucchini and trim ends. Slice zucchini lengthwise about ¼ inch thick.

Spread 1 tablespoon oil in the bottom of a 9-by-13-inch baking dish or similar-size casserole. Cover the bottom with a layer of zucchini slices. Scatter them with half the minced garlic, half the cheese and half the bread crumbs. Drizzle with ½ tablespoon oil. Repeat, layering zucchini, garlic, cheese and bread crumbs, ending with a drizzle of remaining ½ tablespoon oil. Bake for 20 minutes, or until zucchini is tender.

Serves 4. ~ Serve as a side dish with noodles or rice dishes or as part of a vegetable plate with sautéed potato cubes and sliced tomatoes.

Broiled Tomatoes

TOP-QUALITY FRUITS and vegetables don't require a lot of work to make them great eating. These tomatoes are simply split and broiled with herbed bread crumbs on top.

1 tablespoon olive oil or vegetable oil
1 large garlic clove, left whole
⅔ cup dry bread crumbs
½ teaspoon dried basil or tarragon
½ teaspoon dried thyme leaves
½ teaspoon salt
½ teaspoon freshly ground pepper
2 large ripe tomatoes, cored and halved

All broiler units are different; watch the tomatoes and adjust the timing, if necessary.

Preheat the broiler and put the oven rack in the middle of the oven (or if you have a separate broiler unit, move the pan as far away from the flames as you can).

Heat oil in a wide skillet and add garlic. Cook over medium heat, until garlic begins to brown, about 5 minutes or so.

Remove and discard garlic and add bread crumbs and basil or tarragon, thyme, salt and pepper. Cook bread crumbs, stirring, until they darken a little and smell toasty, about 5 minutes.

Place tomatoes on a pie pan or other similar-size baking dish. Divide crumb mixture evenly among 4 tomato halves. Broil for about 10 minutes, or until tomatoes have softened and crumbs have formed a crust.

Serves 4. ~ Serve as part of a simple vegetable plate with Kale and Currants (page 158) and couscous or rice, or as a side dish with Cheese Grits (page 137), Greek-Style Noodles (page 104) or Barley-Mushroom Pilaf (page 139).

Roasted Vegetable Mélange

ROASTED VEGETABLES are pillars of vegetarian cuisine. They are simple, come together quickly, go with just about anything, taste fabulous and make great leftovers. And have I mentioned they're good for you? Roasted vegetables need a little bit of oil coating, which absorbs and holds heat, allowing the vegetables to brown. Add a little more oil if you feel indulgent.

Leftovers can be seasoned with a little vinegar and served cold or at room temperature as a salad, or they can be chopped into small pieces and tossed with hot noodles or stirred into Quicker Tomato Sauce (page 108).

½ pound fresh mushrooms
2 red or green bell peppers
1 small eggplant
1 medium onion
2 tablespoons olive oil
1 teaspoon salt
½ teaspoon freshly ground pepper

Preheat the oven to 400 degrees.

Clean mushrooms and trim woody stems. Core bell peppers, cut them into quarters lengthwise and put them in a large bowl. Peel eggplant only if you want to, cut it into larger-than-bite-size cubes and put in the bowl. Cut onion into quarters and place in the bowl. Add mushrooms, oil, salt and pepper and toss to coat.

Spread vegetables on a lightly greased shallow baking sheet and bake for 20 minutes, stirring once or twice, or until they are tender and beginning to brown.

Serves 4. ~ Serve with plain noodles or rice and rolls.

Pizzas

Restaurant chefs have taught home cooks that pizza doesn't require mozzarella cheese and tomato sauce to fit the definition. From artichokes to pineapple, virtually anything edible qualifies as topping and any cheese is fair game.

The universal link of all pizzas is bread dough of some sort, but even there, different cooks experiment, so the line between what's foccacia (an Italian flatbread) or a Mexican quesadilla and what's pizza begins to blur.

Although my children have tired of delivered pizza, they continue to love homemade versions, particularly if they have a hand in making them—we can decrease the amount of cheese on my daughter's portion, leave the mushrooms off my son's and make garlic sticks with a pinch of leftover dough.

If you make your own pizza a couple of times, it will become easier and easier. Pretty

soon your children will help, it will become a little family ritual and, though not quick, will be an entirely pleasant experience.

The first 10 of my pizza-making years I had neither a round pan nor a pizza cutter. Some people have fancy pizza stones and they make fabulous crust, but not having gadgets is no reason to skip making pizza.

Here's how to make pizza better, easier or quicker with what you have in your cabinets:

- Mozzarella is not your only cheese option, so there's no reason to make a special trip to the supermarket for the "right" cheese. In fact, I prefer provolone but often use a mixture of cheeses that might be handy, including smoked or regular Cheddar, Monterey Jack (with or without jalapeño bits) or even feta cheese.

- Use fresh sliced tomatoes, cherry tomato halves or a store-bought spaghetti sauce in a jar as your tomato layer.

- If you're ready to tackle your own pizza dough, remember that you can make it in the morning, cover with plastic wrap and refrigerate it until dinnertime. It still rises, but much slower.

- If you're the kind of cook who plans ahead, buy frozen bread dough. A loaf of dough will thaw and rise from morning until dinnertime, when you can flatten it into pizza crust. Place the frozen dough in a large bowl, brush with a little oil and cover with plastic wrap. It should thaw and rise in about 8 hours.

- Leave the tomato sauce off entirely and smear the dough with olive oil. Then sprinkle with chopped garlic, cheese and other toppings. Or use sliced fresh tomatoes, sprinkle with fresh herbs and forgo the cheese altogether.

Pizzas

Cheesy Thin-Crust Pizza

These hybrids of pizza and quesadillas dripping with cheese are a cinch to prepare and cook quickly. The thin tortillas will cook unevenly, with crispy brown patches here and there. That's okay; it adds to the charm.

- **2** 12-inch flour tortillas
- **¾-1** cup grated sharp Cheddar cheese
- **¾-1** cup prepared spaghetti sauce or pizza sauce
- **½** green or red bell pepper, thinly sliced
- **¼** cup sliced green olives or pitted imported black olives
- **1** cup grated fontina or provolone cheese (about ¼ pound)

> Keep flour tortillas in the freezer, thawing them as you need them (flour tortillas can be refrozen after thawing).

Preheat the oven to 400 degrees.

Lay 1 tortilla on a pizza pan and scatter half the Cheddar cheese over it. Spread on a tablespoon or two of spaghetti sauce or pizza sauce. Top with second tortilla. Spread on remaining sauce, then scatter peppers and olives over top. Scatter with remaining Cheddar and fontina or provolone.

Bake for 20 minutes, or until cheese bubbles.

Serves 2. ~ Serve with roasted or grilled zucchini or steamed asparagus.

Simple Pizza

FOR THOSE WHO ARE INTIMIDATED by yeast, pizza dough is a good place to practice. It's a small amount, there are few ingredients and technique isn't so critical—everyone loves the final product.

Basic dough has only four ingredients besides water. I've added sugar to the recipe below to give the yeast a ready source of food so the dough rises faster. If you have loads of time to let the dough rise, omit it. Though many pizza doughs call for oil, this one doesn't. Feel free to add a tablespoon to the dough mixture, if you prefer. Customize the pizza by adding your favorite toppings—mushrooms, olives, green pepper, for instance.

Dough

- 2½ cups all-purpose flour
- 1 teaspoon sugar
- 1 package active dry yeast
- ½ teaspoon salt
- 1 cup minus 2 tablespoons hot tap water

Topping

- 1 tablespoon olive oil or vegetable oil
- 3 garlic cloves, minced
- 1 8-ounce can tomato sauce
- ½ teaspoon dried basil
- ½ teaspoon dried oregano
- 1½-2 cups grated cheese (I prefer provolone; mozzarella also works well)

• • •

You can use spaghetti sauce from a jar if you want to save time.

• • •

To make dough: In a medium bowl, combine flour, sugar, yeast and salt with a wooden spoon. Stir to mix, then add hot tap water and stir well. Use your hands when dough gets too stiff to stir with the spoon. Fold and flatten dough repeatedly, adding flour if mixture gets sticky. When dough is smooth, form it into a ball and place it in the bowl. Set the bowl in a sink containing 2 inches of hottest tap water. It can stay there for as little as 10 minutes and for up to 1 hour.

Preheat the oven to 500 degrees.

To make topping: In a small pan, heat oil over medium heat. Add garlic and, when it begins to color, about 1 minute, add tomato sauce, basil and oregano. Cook for 1 minute, then set aside.

To assemble and bake: Generously grease 1 or 2 pizza pans, a baking sheet or a shallow roasting pan (I use a shallow roasting pan 15½ by 11 inches). Stretch or press dough into desired thickness. Cover with tomato sauce to within ½ inch of the edge. Sprinkle with cheese.

Place pan on the bottom rack of the oven and bake until cheese browns and bubbles, about 15 minutes.

Serves 4.

Pizza Crust Mix

ONE OF MY FRIENDS made at least one pizza a week when she had teenagers living in the house. She premixed a large amount of pizza crust mix, then she—or the teens—could simply mix it with water.

I use unbleached flour in this recipe. If you use all-purpose, you may need to add a little more after you stir in the water so the dough isn't too sticky. That's because all-purpose flour contains less protein than unbleached and absorbs less water.

5 pounds all-purpose flour (about 20 cups) or half whole-wheat flour and half all-purpose
6 packages rapid-rise yeast (about 5 tablespoons)
6 teaspoons sugar
4 teaspoons salt

Combine all ingredients in a large bowl. Use a spoon, whisk or your hands to mix ingredients together. Mix thoroughly.

Place mixture in a canister or zipper-style plastic bag and store in the refrigerator for up to 3 months (yeast keeps better if chilled). (If you want mix to last 4 to 6 months, store at least part of it in the freezer.)

To make pizza crust: Mix 3¾ cups pizza mix with 1½ cups water. Mix with a spoon, then knead with your hands, adding a little flour if the dough is sticky after it has been thoroughly blended. Knead for about 10 minutes, folding dough over, pressing it to flatten, then folding it again; it

should be smooth but not sticky. Place dough in a bowl and cover with plastic wrap. Set the bowl in a sink filled with 2 inches of hottest tap water and allow it to rise for 30 minutes while you prepare toppings and sauces.

To bake pizza: Preheat the oven to 500 degrees (or the hottest setting up to that). Generously grease 2 pizza pans (12-inch diameter) or a baking sheet or sheets.

Divide dough in half and stretch, press or roll it to an even thickness to fit your pan (the 12-inch dough round will be about ¼ inch thick, bigger pans will yield a thinner-crust pizza). Make the outside rim of the pizza a little higher. Cover with tomato sauce, toppings and cheese as desired.

3¾ cups of the mix makes two 12-inch pizzas.
The mix makes 10 to 11 round pizzas, each 12 inches in diameter.

Greek Pita Pizza

PITA BREAD ROUNDS help you get dinner to the table almost instantly because the topping ingredients are tossed together in one bowl. Almost no skill is required. One caveat: Pita breads differ in both diameter and thickness. Don't drive far and wide for a 6-inch pita when your store sells 7-inch ones, but be mentally prepared for a change in cooking time. The same is true of thick vs. thin crusts. The vegetables in the topping don't cook to mushy softness; they remain crisp, though the cheese should melt. This is a knife-and-fork meal.

4 6-inch pita breads, sliced horizontally to form thin disks
About 1 teaspoon oregano
1 8-ounce can tomato sauce
½ pound provolone or mozzarella cheese or cheese of your choice, grated
1 6-ounce jar marinated artichoke hearts, drained and chopped
½ medium onion, chopped (about ½ cup)
1 red, yellow or green bell pepper, seeded and chopped small (about 1 cup)
¼ cup sliced black or green olives

These pizzas are not super-cheesy.
Add more cheese if you like.

Preheat the oven to 450 degrees.

Place pita breads on an ungreased baking sheet and bake for 5 to 7 minutes to crisp.

Meanwhile, stir oregano into tomato sauce can. Toss cheese, artichoke hearts, onion, pepper and olives briefly in a bowl to combine.

Remove pitas from the oven and spread with a thin layer of tomato sauce (you may have a little left over). Divide the topping among the 8 bread halves.

Bake for 5 to 10 minutes, until cheese is melted, bread is toasty and vegetables are warmed through. Serve hot.

Serves 4. ~ Serve with sliced cantaloupe or Quick Fried Squash (page 162).

Burritos & Sandwiches

THE BEST THINGS come in small packages, and that includes food. Tell your 8-year-old he's having bean sprouts, cabbage and bits of tofu in bean sauce and he'll join the circus or, at the very least, whine. Tell him you're having egg rolls and he'll be delighted.

Empanadas, turnovers, calzones, sandwiches—you name it—food always tastes better in a bundle, and not just to children. I can't think of a food package I don't like. Some of those little bundles require huge time commitments, however. Making egg rolls is almost a full-day project for me.

But others make quick dinners. One of

my favorite meals is a sandwich of sautéed onions and bell peppers seasoned with hot sauce and served on toasted buns, perhaps with a little provolone or, if I'm lucky, goat cheese from a nearby dairy.

If family members are suspicious of food, packaging helps make the meal successful. I'm not sure my kids would willingly eat scrambled eggs, salsa and potatoes, but they like the mixture rolled and baked in a corn tortilla. My brother became a vegetarian in 1972, but he didn't start eating beans until 10 years later. His crossover dish was bean burritos—with plenty of cheese and sour cream, to be sure, but now he loves beans.

Pita bread pockets, corn and flour tortillas, sliced bread and buns are all kept handy in my house—often in the freezer if I think I can't use them quickly.

Here are some likely candidates for stuffing food wrappers:

- Mix leftover marinated vegetables (such as Greek Peasant Salad, page 20) with beans or cheese and use the mixture to stuff pita bread.

- Roast vegetables, such as potatoes, eggplant and carrots, lightly coated with a little olive oil. Cut the roasted pieces small and coat them with bottled or homemade salsa. Put into warmed flour or corn tortillas. Or fill with Roasted Vegetable Mélange (page 165).

- Grilled marinated eggplant, onions and peppers make irresistible fillings for sandwich buns. If you're cooking outside, make extra and serve the leftovers the next day, stacked on a Kaiser bun with sliced tomatoes and perhaps some fresh herbs, a smear of pesto or some soft baked garlic. If it's too cold to fire up the grill or takes too long, substitute broiled marinated vegetables or lightly sautéed mixtures.

burritos & Sandwiches

Quick Cheese Burritos

THIS DISH seems to have universal appeal, and is especially popular with teenagers, even if they aren't vegetarian. Think of it as a Mexican variation on stuffed manicotti or pasta shells.

- **1** large egg
- **1** 15-ounce container ricotta cheese (part-skim works well)
- **2** cups grated Monterey Jack cheese (about ½ pound)
- **2** bunches green onions, trimmed and chopped (about 1 cup)
- **1** 2¼-ounce can sliced black olives, drained
- **1** teaspoon ground cumin
- **½** teaspoon salt
- **1** cup bottled salsa or enchilada sauce, or to taste
- **10** 8-inch flour tortillas

> I always prefer imported brine-cured olives in cooking except here, where canned California olives work better.

Preheat the oven to 400 degrees. Butter a 9-by-13-inch baking pan or a wide casserole dish.

Beat egg in a medium-size bowl. Add ricotta, 1½ cups grated Monterey Jack, green onions, olives, cumin and salt. Stir to mix completely.

Pour about ½ cup salsa into the bottom of the casserole and tip it to coat the bottom.

Spoon about 3 tablespoons ricotta-cheese mixture across the middle of each tortilla. Roll tortilla to enclose filling and place it in the pan seam side down. Repeat with remaining tortillas. Pour remaining ½ cup salsa over tortillas and sprinkle with remaining cheese.

Bake for 20 minutes, or until burritos are hot throughout and cheese on top is melted.

Serves 4 or 5. ~ Serve with a simple green salad.

Black Bean Burritos

TOASTING GARLIC AND SPICES gives a whole new flavor dimension to black bean burritos. My son, who's never met a burger he didn't like, picked up this burrito with his hands and said, "Mmmmmmm . . . meat!" I'm not sure if that's good or bad.

One half of a seeded jalapeño pepper does not make a very hot filling. If you like more heat, add more pepper and a few of the seeds.

- 3 large garlic cloves, unpeeled and left whole
- 1 teaspoon ground cumin
- 1 teaspoon dried oregano
- 1 14½-ounce can diced tomatoes
- ½ jalapeño pepper, or to taste (seeded, if desired)
- ½ teaspoon salt
- 3 16-ounce cans black beans
- 10 8-inch wheat tortillas
- 1 cup grated Cheddar cheese
- Sour cream and/or salsa (optional)

You can make the filling ahead and refrigerate it or freeze it, but it will thicken quite a bit. Thin it with water, vegetable broth or tomato juice.

Preheat the oven to 400 degrees and grease a 9-by-13-inch baking dish or similar-size casserole.

Heat garlic cloves in a dry skillet over medium heat for 15 minutes, shaking the skillet occasionally to turn garlic. The skin that touches the skillet will char to a chocolate brown. Reduce the heat if garlic appears to be in danger of burning. When garlic is browned and somewhat soft, remove the skillet from the heat. Remove garlic; set aside. Off the heat, immediately add cumin and oregano to the skillet. Stir a few times to expose it all to the heat.

Meanwhile, combine tomatoes in a blender with jalapeño. Blend for 15 seconds. Peel garlic

cloves when they are cool enough to handle and add them to the blender with toasted cumin and oregano and salt. Blend for 15 more seconds, until smooth.

Drain beans well and put them in the skillet. Add tomato sauce and simmer on medium heat to thicken, about 15 or 20 minutes. Sauce will be lumpy because of beans but thick enough to stay where you put it in a tortilla.

As beans thicken, heat tortillas until they are warm and flexible. There are several ways to warm them. You can do it over a gas flame, in the microwave, in a dry skillet or in the oven. I do it over a flame by laying 1 tortilla directly on a burning flame and turning it with tongs every 2 seconds, until warm and getting brown spots. If you have an electric stove, put a dry skillet on high heat and warm 1 tortilla at a time by turning every few seconds. To microwave, wrap tortillas in a damp cloth and microwave on medium power for 1 minute. Change the position of the tortillas in the stack, putting the center ones on top and bottom, and microwave for 30 seconds more. Or wrap in aluminum foil and place them in a 400-degree oven for 15 minutes.

Spread a generous ¼ cup of bean mixture across 1 tortilla in a long strip. Roll tortilla up to enclose filling. Place in the casserole, seam side down. Repeat with remaining tortillas. Sprinkle with cheese and bake for 15 minutes, or until cheese is melted and burritos are hot throughout. Serve with sour cream and/or salsa, if desired.

Serves 4 to 5. ~ Serve with Honey-Mustard Carrot Salad (page 26) or Savory Broccoli Salad (page 28).

Potato and Egg Tortillas

BREAKFAST BURRITOS are wildly popular in restaurants. But big breakfasts become dinners at our house. In the morning, we do easier, quicker things like toast or bagels.

4 tablespoons olive oil or vegetable oil
1 pound potatoes (preferably new potatoes)
1 small onion, chopped
3 large eggs
1 teaspoon salt
½ teaspoon freshly ground pepper
12 6-inch corn tortillas
¼ pound shredded Monterey Jack cheese
About 1 cup bottled salsa

Preheat the oven to 450 degrees. Grease a 9-by-13-inch baking pan (or similar-size casserole dish) with 2 tablespoons oil. (You need all this oil to make the tortillas bake crispy.)

Chop potatoes in small dice (about ½ inch), peeling them only if desired. The smaller the potato pieces, the less time required to cook them. Heat remaining 2 tablespoons oil in a wide skillet over medium-high heat. Add potatoes to the skillet.

Add onions and cook, stirring, until potatoes are tender, about 20 minutes.

Combine eggs, salt and pepper in a small bowl and beat well. Add eggs to the skillet and cook until nearly firm, about 3 to 4 minutes.

Heat another wide skillet over high heat. Place a corn tortilla in the skillet and warm it for about 15 seconds, flipping it once or twice. It should be warm through and pliable. Repeat with remaining tortillas, stacking them so they retain their heat and stay soft. (You shouldn't have to wash the pan afterward.)

Fill each corn tortilla by putting about 3 tablespoons egg-potato mixture down the center, then sprinkle with a little cheese and salsa. Roll it tightly. Place, seam side down, in the baking dish, cover with foil and bake for 10 to 15 minutes, or until cheese is melted. Serve with more salsa, if desired.

Serves 4 to 6. ~ Serve with steamed asparagus or asparagus cut into 2-inch lengths and sautéed with garlic and olive oil.

Corn tortillas can be frustrating to roll—they crack—but keep them moist with salsa and cover them during part of cooking and they'll turn out just fine.

Cheese and Vegetable Sandwich

THIS IS ONE of my favorite foods. It tastes great, travels well and even improves if wrapped tightly in plastic wrap and given a few hours to sit at room temperature. Exact measurements are hard to quantify. I've used round sandwich buns, the longer hoagie buns and even French bread loaves cut into sandwich-size sections. The combination even works on sturdy sliced bread.

2 large green or red bell peppers
2-3 tablespoons olive oil
1 red onion
Hot pepper sauce (optional)
Salt and freshly ground pepper to taste
4 large sandwich buns
¼-½ pound provolone, Havarti or Cheddar cheese

> **This sandwich tastes great with nearly any kind of cheese, from supermarket cream cheese to crumbly goat cheese.**

Core and slice peppers. Heat oil in a wide skillet and add peppers. Cook over medium heat as you prepare onion. Slice onion about ⅛ inch thick and add to the skillet. Cook over medium heat, stirring occasionally, until vegetables are limp and beginning to brown. Season with hot pepper sauce (if using), salt and pepper.

Split sandwich buns in half horizontally. Divide cheese among bottom halves of buns. Top with some vegetable mixture. Close up sandwiches, cut in half and serve.

Serves 4. ~ Serve with marinated cherry tomatoes and roasted potatoes cut into long wedges, tossed with olive oil and baked at 425 degrees for 25 minutes, or until golden.

Cheesy Quesadillas

Moms in the 1950s made grilled cheese sandwiches to go with soups. Cooks in the 1990s are more apt to make quesadillas. Flour tortillas come in all sizes, so be ready to adapt the recipe, using more if they're 6-inch, fewer if they're 10-inch.

8 8-inch flour tortillas
1 cup grated sharp Cheddar or Monterey Jack cheese
1 4-ounce jar chopped pimientos
Several jalapeño pepper slices to taste

Preheat the oven to 350 degrees.

Place 4 tortillas on a baking sheet. Divide grated cheese among them.

Scatter pimientos and jalapeño slices over cheese. Top with remaining tortilla and press firmly.

Bake for about 8 minutes, or until light brown.

Serves 4. ~ Serve with soup or a piece of fruit.

Add cooked black beans and you'll make the quesadillas more filling.

My Hero

• • • • • • • •

IF YOU'RE FAMILIAR with the New Orleans muffaletta sandwich, you know about the pickly-olivy relish that makes it so savory. It's the best part of the sandwich as far as I'm concerned, so I make a meatless hero with a muffaletta-style relish. Use leftover relish for sandwiches (it keeps forever in the refrigerator), sprinkle it over lettuce or cold vegetables or stir it into leftover navy beans or chick-peas to make a cold salad.

Relish

- 1 cup chopped olives, green or imported black or a mixture of both
- ½ cup chopped peperoncini pickles
- 2 tablespoons capers
- ¼ cup olive oil
- 2 tablespoons vinegar (any kind)
- 1 teaspoon dried oregano
- 2 large garlic cloves, minced

Sandwiches

- 4 French rolls or two 8-ounce French loaves
- 1 red or green bell pepper, cored and sliced
- ½ red onion, thinly sliced
- ½ cucumber, peeled and sliced
- ½ tomato, thinly sliced
- ¼ pound smoked aged cheese (such as Cheddar or provolone) or cheese of your choice

• • •

Peperoncini are small pickled peppers, not really hot. They and the capers are found near the other pickles at your supermarket.

• • •

To make relish: Combine olives and pickles with capers, olive oil, vinegar, oregano and garlic. Set aside.

To make sandwiches: Slice rolls or French bread in half horizontally. Layer with a few slices of bell pepper, a slice of red onion, some cucumber, tomato and cheese. Dress with olive relish (you'll have leftovers). Serve immediately or wrap tightly in plastic wrap, refrigerate and serve later at room temperature.

Serves 4. ~ Serve with roasted potato wedges or Dusted Potatoes (page 75).

Savory Chick-Pea Pita Pockets

HERE'S A CHICK-PEA salad that stands in for tuna. As with tuna, you can bind it with mayonnaise (instead of olive oil and lemon juice) or you can add pickle relish (or diced peperoncini) or minced celery. To make this without cheese, add ½ cup salted, toasted sunflower seeds and ¼ cup minced green olives. Serve as a filling for pita pockets or as a stuffing for hollowed-out fresh tomato halves.

- ¼ cup sesame seeds
- ½ cup minced fresh parsley
- 1 teaspoon dried basil
- 1 large bell pepper, cored and finely chopped (about 1½ cups)
- 2 garlic cloves, minced
- 3 tablespoons olive oil
- 3 tablespoons lemon juice
- ¼ teaspoon crushed red pepper
- 1 16-ounce can chick-peas (also called garbanzo beans)
- 2-4 ounces feta cheese (½-1 cup crumbled)
- Salt and freshly ground pepper to taste
- 6-8 6-inch pita breads

You can substitute toasted hulled sunflower seeds (salted or unsalted) for sesame seeds.

Preheat the oven to 350 degrees.

Put sesame seeds in a shallow pan, such as a pie pan, and toast in the oven for 15 minutes, or until they are golden brown and smell aromatic.

Meanwhile, combine parsley in a medium bowl with basil. Add peppers, garlic, oil, lemon juice, crushed red pepper.

Drain chick-peas completely, chop them coarsely and add to the bowl along with feta and toasted sesame seeds. Toss to combine and season with salt and pepper.

Slice pita breads in half, open their pockets and fill with about ¼ cup chick-pea salad.

Makes 3½ cups filling; 12-16 pita halves.

Breads

BAKING BREAD FOR DINNER is right above winning the lottery on the highly improbable list. Most people don't bake it on a leisurely Saturday afternoon, much less on a rushed weeknight.

Still, taking some care with bread at dinner has its benefits, not the least of which is how pampered your guests will feel when you serve something warm from the oven. Guests in this case may mean children, who might be less inclined to gripe about dinner if they see hot bread along with it.

Sometimes hot bread at our house is nothing more than a toasted English muffin half with melted cheese on it. That's a standard accompaniment to vegetable soup. Sometimes it's store-bought rolls or bread, split in half and smeared with garlic butter, perhaps topped with cheese. Simple as that sounds, it's a favorite with family and friends. Or sometimes, hot bread—like

Bruschetta with Roasted Garlic and Capers (page 193)—becomes the most interesting part of the meal, served to make leftovers more exciting. My bruschetta uses firm bread as a sort of pizza crust and is topped with cherry tomatoes and roasted garlic. Bruschetta toppings are as varied as pizza toppings—or even more so.

For slightly more elaborate occasions, baking powder and baking soda give rising power to quick breads, like corn bread and biscuits. Yeast takes a little longer, but this book provides you with one yeasted offering that doesn't take skill or much time to bake: Breadsticks (page 194).

When you gain confidence with these recipes, go on and experiment with others. Bread always makes the meal.

breads

Bruschetta with Roasted Garlic and Capers

GIVING A PRECISE SIZE for the bread used in bruschetta is somewhat beside the point. Bruschetta is one way to use up European-style bread that is beginning to stale. It might be a baguette that's beyond the pale or a boule that needs to be finished off.

My vision of the right size for bruschetta is the size of a man's hand. Whether that hand belongs to Michael Jordan or Mickey Rooney doesn't much matter. With cooking, flexibility is key. Think of bruschetta as a hearty accompaniment to an otherwise light meal (soup or salad).

6 large garlic cloves
1 tablespoon olive oil
4 slices firm European-style bread, about 4 by 6 inches and ¾ inch thick
2 tablespoons capers
1-2 ripe tomatoes, sliced
Salt and freshly ground pepper

• • •

If your tomatoes aren't ripe, omit or use canned, drained.

• • •

Preheat the oven to 350 degrees.

Peel garlic cloves and place in a small baking dish or pie pan with olive oil. Bake for 15 minutes, stirring once or twice, until garlic softens and begins to brown.

Meanwhile, slice bread and toast it (on both sides if they are slices, on the top side if it is a horizontally cut baguette).

When garlic is done, mash it in the pan with a fork. Stir in capers and then smear the whole mixture over top of toast. Top with tomato slices. Season with salt and pepper to taste and serve.

Serves 4 as a side dish. ~ Serve with soup or salad, or as a light meal accompanied by fresh melon or grapes.

Breadsticks

Breadsticks do require working with yeast, but you don't need skill and the bread doesn't have to rise. The first time around, make these when you aren't too rushed. Once you get the rhythm, you can make them with your eyes closed. They taste good sprinkled with poppy seeds, sesame seeds or coarse salt (regular shaker salt dissolves on the bread).

- 2½ cups all-purpose flour or bread flour, plus more if needed
- 1 package (2½ teaspoons) rapid-rise yeast
- 1 teaspoon salt
- 1 teaspoon sugar
- 1 tablespoon olive oil
- 1 cup hot water
- Coarse salt, poppy seeds or sesame seeds (optional)
- Egg white (optional)

• • •

You can also make breadsticks with thawed frozen bread dough.

• • •

Preheat the oven to 450 degrees.

Combine flour, yeast, salt, sugar, oil and water in a large bowl. Stir with a wooden spoon to combine, then use your hands, if necessary, to mix dough evenly.

Once dough has come together, transfer to a lightly floured countertop. To knead, press down on dough, fold it over, turn it, flatten it again, and repeat until all ingredients are evenly blended and mixture is smooth and not very sticky, for about 4 minutes. Add more flour, if necessary, to keep dough from sticking.

Roll on the counter or between your hands into a log about 2 inches in diameter and cut into portions about 1 inch long. Roll little dough hunks to about twice the thickness of a pencil. If dough shrinks back as you roll it, set it aside for a few minutes to relax it, so it will be easier to roll. Place on a greased baking sheet, leaving 1 inch between the sticks.

Sprinkle breadsticks with salt or seeds, if desired (you may need to brush breadsticks with beaten egg white to get seeds to stick).

Bake for 10 to 15 minutes, depending on the thickness, or until lightly browned and cooked through. Serve hot. Store leftover breadsticks at room temperature and reheat in a 325-degree oven for about 10 minutes.

Makes about 16 breadsticks. ~ Serve with soup, noodle dishes or wherever hot bread is appropriate. These are good with or without butter.

Garlic (Cheese) Bread

THIS IS OUR MOST FREQUENT ACCOMPANIMENT to vegetable meals. If I have Romano cheese, I grate it in large shreds—not fine powder—and sprinkle it on the toast for grown-ups. A sprinkling of Parmesan, fontina or provolone would also taste good. My kids prefer plain garlic toast.

2 French rolls or hoagie buns
2 garlic cloves, minced
1-2 tablespoons softened butter or olive oil
2-3 tablespoons grated cheese (optional)

Preheat the broiler, with a rack 4 inches from the heat.

Halve bread horizontally. Broil until toasty but only barely browned, about ½ to 1 minute.

Mash together garlic and butter or combine garlic and oil.

When rolls are toasty, spread butter or brush oil over them. Sprinkle with cheese, if desired. Broil again until medium brown, about 30 seconds; watch carefully. Serve immediately.

Serves 4 to 6.

Cheese-Mustard Muffins

OFTEN MUFFINS ARE TOO RICH and sweet to go with dinner foods. But vegetable plates sometimes want for substantial accompaniments, and cheese muffins fill the bill. Besides, they are easy to make.

2 cups all-purpose flour
2 teaspoons baking powder
¼ teaspoon salt
¼ teaspoon freshly ground pepper
1¼ cups milk
¼ cup melted butter or vegetable oil
1 cup grated sharp Cheddar cheese
2 tablespoons honey or sugar
1 large egg
1 teaspoon Dijon-style or any European-style mustard

Preheat the oven to 400 degrees. Butter a 12-cup muffin tin.

Combine flour, baking powder, salt and pepper on a plate or sheet of wax paper.

In a medium-size bowl, beat together milk, butter or oil, cheese, honey or sugar, egg and mustard. Stir in dry ingredients until barely blended.

Divide among the muffin cups and bake for 20 minutes, until golden brown.

Makes 12 muffins. ~ Serve with simple meals like a vegetable plate with baked potato, sliced tomatoes and Quick Fried Cabbage (page 160). They are also good with soup or salad meals.

Simple Corn Bread

Corn bread is a quick, easy dinner bread. It seems to taste best with bean dishes and doesn't go well at all with pasta. I don't ever put sugar in corn bread served for dinner, but some people like their bread with a little sweetener. If you do, add 1 tablespoon sugar with the cornmeal. The following recipe—which requires no wheat flour—uses the old Southern technique of baking the corn bread in a hot cast-iron skillet. If you don't have one, use an 8-inch-square baking pan.

Split leftover corn bread in half horizontally, butter it and toast it under the broiler. Top with hot chili or black beans and a little grated cheese.

If you don't have buttermilk and/or baking soda, substitute 1 cup regular milk and 1 teaspoon baking powder.

- **2 tablespoons vegetable oil**
- **1 large egg**
- **1 teaspoon salt**
- **½ teaspoon baking soda**
- **1 cup yellow cornmeal**
- **1 cup buttermilk**

Preheat the oven to 425 degrees.

If you're using an 8- or 9-inch cast-iron skillet, put 1 tablespoon of oil in it and set it in the oven. If you're using an 8-inch square pan, oil it but don't preheat it.

Beat egg. Add salt and baking soda and beat. Stir in cornmeal, buttermilk and remaining 1 tablespoon oil. Stir to combine. Use a pot holder to remove the hot skillet from the oven and pour batter into it.

Bake for 20 minutes, or until corn bread is deep brown around the edges. Cut into wedges or squares.

Serves 6.

Green Chili-Corn Muffins

Beer gives these muffins yeasty undertones, while the cheese makes them tender and moist. They are not at all spicy, though the green chilies lend a Southwestern flavor. If you'd like to add a little heat, use Monterey Jack cheese studded with bits of jalapeño pepper.

2 cups all-purpose flour
1 cup yellow cornmeal
2 teaspoons baking powder
1 teaspoon salt
1 large egg
1½ cups beer
1 4-ounce can chopped mild green chilies
1 cup coarsely grated Cheddar cheese
1 tablespoon vegetable oil

Preheat the oven to 375 degrees. Butter a 12-cup muffin tin.

Combine flour, cornmeal, baking powder and salt on a plate or wax paper.

Beat egg in a medium bowl. Add beer, chilies, cheese and oil. Stir briefly to blend, then stir in cornmeal mixture until just barely moistened. Batter will be thick.

Divide batter among the muffin cups—they will fill to the brim.

Bake for 20 minutes, or until browned and cooked through.

Makes 12 muffins. ~ **Serve hot with soup or salad meals or with bean main dishes.**

Biscuits

I KNOW THAT USING a rolling pin can seem an insurmountable obstacle to timid cooks contemplating biscuits. There is such a thing as drop biscuits, but rolled ones are ever so much better. If you don't have a rolling pin, use a wine bottle or plastic liter bottle: Biscuits don't require much rolling and this dough is so tender that it complies easily.

- **1¾ cups all-purpose flour**
- **2½ teaspoons baking powder**
- **¾ teaspoon salt**
- **6 tablespoons butter or shortening or a combination**
- **¾ cup milk (skim is fine)**

Preheat the oven to 450 degrees.

Combine flour, baking powder and salt in a medium bowl.

Add butter or shortening and use 2 knives or a pastry blender to cut it into flour until mixture resembles coarse meal. Add milk and use a fork to blend. This takes just a few swift strokes; dough will look shaggy.

> **Cutting butter into flour means crossing the 2 knives against each other to make an X, then pulling out toward the sides of the bowl. Do it again and again until the butter is in little bits.**

Sprinkle a little flour on your countertop and place dough on top. Sprinkle a little flour on dough and fold dough over. Press down and fold over again 5 or 6 times, until the shagginess has smoothed out.

Roll out dough ¾ inch thick. Cut into biscuits with a 2-inch biscuit cutter or a small juice glass. Place rounds in an ungreased 9-inch cake pan. Press any remaining dough scraps together, knead briefly and roll again. Cut into biscuits and place in the pan.

Bake for 12 minutes, or until biscuits are high and brown on top. Serve hot.

Makes 9 or 10 biscuits. ~ Leftovers can be sliced in half, spread with butter, sprinkled with cinnamon sugar and broiled for breakfast.

Desserts

Americans have a habit of blaming dessert for all our health woes when, in fact, only a small part of the problems we suffer are on account of homemade sweets. Much of the fat we consume comes from cheese, salad dressings and prepackaged pastries (not to mention meat).

I wouldn't rationalize eating a gooey dessert—homemade or otherwise—for dinner every night, even if we think we've been "good" all day by choosing low-fat foods. Since most of us eat vegetarian foods for health reasons, it makes no sense to "reward" ourselves with choices that negate the benefits.

If you find yourself in the firm grip of your sweet tooth, satisfy it by going to some trouble to find great fruit. As a rule, it isn't found at the supermarket. Frequent your local farmers' markets or special produce markets for great plums, peaches, melons

and berries in the summer, apples and pears in the fall, citrus, kiwi and dates in the winter, strawberries and more citrus in the spring.

TRY MAKING FRUIT into something a little more elaborate—bake an apple, poach a pear, stew some dried fruit into compote, whip some berries into mousse. Serve it with candied ginger or sweetened yogurt. And make extra; it'll be a great breakfast in the morning.

But of course, there are other circumstances besides simple desire that require dessert. You're asked to contribute to a potluck or you prepare a special meal that deserves a special finale. This selection is a miscellaneous collection of tried-and-true successes. When I bake, I want recipes I can prepare blindfolded. These qualify.

desserts

Honey Yogurt Sauce

(for strawberries)

THE BEST WAY to eat strawberries is plain. But if you want to make dessert for company, whip up this easy yogurt sauce. Change it to suit your taste by substituting a teaspoon of freshly grated ginger or lemon zest for the nutmeg. If there are leftovers from dinner, eat them for breakfast.

I also love this sauce on winter fruit compotes made by simmering dried fruits in tea or orange juice.

1 8-ounce container plain yogurt
1 tablespoon honey or sugar
⅛ teaspoon vanilla
⅛ teaspoon grated nutmeg

Stir yogurt until creamy. Stir in honey or sugar, vanilla and nutmeg until blended.

Makes about 1 cup, enough for 1 pint of strawberries.

Variations

Honey-Lime Yogurt Sauce: Add grated zest and juice of 1 lime to yogurt. Taste. If it's too tart, add a little more honey. Serve with cantaloupe, blackberries or mixed fresh-fruit compote.

Honey-Lemon Yogurt Sauce: Substitute grated zest of ½ lemon for the nutmeg.

Baked Apples

I CORE APPLES by going halfway into them with a paring knife, then digging out the seeds with a grapefruit spoon. If you're shy on utensils, just cut the apples vertically in half and dig out the cores. If you have leftover apples and refrigerate them, your sauce may turn sugary. The crystals should dissolve on reheating.

4 tart apples (such as Granny Smith)
¼ cup light or dark brown sugar
1 teaspoon ground cinnamon
2 tablespoons chopped pecans or walnuts (optional)
¾ cup boiling water
3 tablespoons sugar
1 teaspoon vanilla
Vanilla ice cream, whipped cream, sweetened yogurt or crumbled Praline (opposite page)

> **If you don't have brown sugar, substitute granulated.**

Preheat the oven to 375 degrees.

Wash apples and use a small paring knife to remove their cores to within ½ inch of the bottom. Combine brown sugar, cinnamon and nuts, if using, and fill centers of apples with mixture.

Stir together water and sugar in an 8-inch baking pan. Place apples upright in the pan.

Bake for 30 minutes, or until apples are tender. Dip a spoon into pan juices and drizzle apples a few times as they cook. Transfer apples to 4 dessert plates. If the sauce isn't thick, pour it into a small saucepan and boil rapidly for a few minutes to reduce it to a thick syrup. Remove from the heat and add vanilla. Spoon over apples.

Serve with ice cream, whipped cream, yogurt or a sprinkling of praline.

Serves 4.

Praline

THIS PRALINE is like peanut brittle and can be eaten like candy. I sprinkle it on poached or baked fruit or ice cream.

1 cup pecans, walnuts or almonds
1 cup sugar

Preheat the oven to 350 degrees.

Spread nuts in a single layer on a baking sheet and toast, stirring occasionally, for 10 minutes, or until they begin to brown and smell toasty. (Toasting time differs with type of nut.) Cool and chop.

Melt sugar in a skillet over low heat, stirring constantly. When it is melted and browned, stir in nuts.

Pour onto an oiled platter, marble or countertop. When cool, crack into pieces. Chop into fine bits with a knife for sprinkling on poached or baked fruit.

Makes about 1 cup.

Caramel Brownies

THE FIRST TIME I tasted one of these brownies, I was warned to pace myself over several hours. They are thin, chewy and very sweet. I like to cut them small—at least 30 to the pan—and eat them only occasionally. That way they don't have to bear a caution from the Surgeon General.

Brownies

- ½ cup (1 stick) butter, melted
- 2 cups light brown sugar
- 2 large eggs
- 1 teaspoon salt
- ½ teaspoon baking soda
- 2 teaspoons vanilla
- 1½ cups all-purpose flour
- ½ cup flaked coconut (optional)
- 1 cup chopped walnuts or pecans

Icing

- ½ cup (1 stick) butter
- ½ cup light brown sugar
- ¼ cup milk
- 1¾-2 cups powdered sugar
- 1 teaspoon vanilla

• • •

If you have leftover nuts that you think you'll be keeping awhile, store them in the freezer. They'll keep longer.

• • •

Preheat the oven to 350 degrees. Lightly butter a 9-by-13-inch baking pan.

To make brownies: Beat butter, brown sugar, eggs, salt, baking soda and vanilla together in a bowl. Stir in flour until completely mixed, then coconut, if using, and nuts. Spread in the baking pan.

Bake for 25 to 30 minutes, or until a toothpick inserted into the center of the pan comes out clean. Brownies will look puffy and lumpy and shouldn't jiggle when you shake the pan. Cool.

Meanwhile, make icing: Melt butter over medium heat in a heavy saucepan. Add brown sugar; stir to blend completely. Remove from the heat and stir for another 2 minutes or so; butter and sugar won't be completely blended, but that's okay. Add milk and stir until sugar dissolves. Add powdered sugar and vanilla and beat to blend. The icing is a little thin at first but firms on standing.

When brownies are cool, spread with icing.

Makes 30 brownies.

Chocolate-Nut Bars

THERE'S NOTHING SUBTLE about a dessert that combines chocolate morsels and nuts. This bar cookie is made of corn syrup, sugar and eggs—a gooey filling that holds the nuts and chips in place. Think of it as little squares of pecan pie liberally studded with chocolate.

Crust

- **1½ cups all-purpose flour**
- **6 tablespoons butter, softened**
- **3 tablespoons sugar**
- **¼ teaspoon salt**

Filling

- **¾ cup sugar**
- **¾ cup corn syrup**
- **1 tablespoon butter, melted**
- **1 teaspoon vanilla or 1 tablespoon bourbon**
- **2 large eggs**
- **1 cup semisweet chocolate chips**
- **1 cup chopped pecans**

Preheat the oven to 350 degrees. Lightly butter a 9-by-13-inch baking pan.

To make crust: Mix flour, butter, sugar and salt in a large bowl, using an electric mixer or your hands (or both), or combine in the bowl of a food processor fitted with a metal blade. Mixture will be crumbly like fine meal. Press it into the pan. Bake for 15 minutes; crust won't be brown.

Meanwhile, make filling: Combine sugar, corn syrup, butter, vanilla or bourbon and eggs in the bowl that you mixed the crust in (no need to wash it). Beat with an electric mixer on low speed until blended, 1 to 2 minutes. Sprinkle chocolate chips and pecans in the bottom of the crust, then pour filling over them.

Bake for 25 minutes, or until filling is set. Cool completely before cutting into squares.

Makes 2 dozen bars.

Variation

Tropical Nut Bars: Substitute 1 cup coconut for chocolate chips. Omit pecans from filling and spread coconut and pecans on crust as you bake crust for 15 minutes, so they toast lightly.

White Chocolate Bars: Replace chocolate chips with ½ cup dried apricots and ½ cup white chocolate chips.

German Apple Cake

THIS RECIPE ISN'T PARTICULARLY FAST TO BAKE—it takes more than an hour—but it requires absolutely no skill. There's no crust to roll, no design to form, no cake to get stuck in the pan. Anybody can do it, and it comes out delicious.

But is it a coffeecake or a dessert? I've used it as both—as dessert for a dinner party, with leftovers for breakfast the next day. It's delicious with ice cream or whipped cream, or with a cup of tea.

Cake

1 cup all-purpose flour
¾ cup plus 2 tablespoons sugar
1 teaspoon baking powder
¼ cup (½ stick) butter, softened
1 teaspoon vanilla
1 large egg
Grated zest of 1 lemon
4-5 large tart apples (such as Granny Smith)

Topping

3 tablespoons butter, melted
3 tablespoons sugar
1 teaspoon vanilla
1 teaspoon ground cinnamon
1 large egg

• • •

This cake can also be made with fresh peaches or plums.

• • •

Preheat the oven to 350 degrees. Butter a 9-inch springform pan or 8-inch square cake pan.

To make cake: Stir flour, sugar and baking powder together in a large bowl. Add butter, vanilla, egg and lemon zest and stir until blended. Pat into the bottom of the pan.

Peel apples, cut them in quarters and remove their cores with a paring knife. Cut apple quarters into slices and put them in an even layer on top of crust.

Bake for 45 minutes, or until browned.

Meanwhile, make topping: Mix all ingredients in a small bowl, stirring to dissolve sugar. Spoon over cake and bake for another 25 to 30 minutes, or until top is firm.

Cool slightly before removing the sides of the pan, if using a springform pan. When cake has cooled a little, cut into wedges or squares. Serve warm or at room temperature.

Makes a 9-inch cake, serves 6 to 8.

Easy Shortbread

THESE EASY AND DELICIOUS SHORTBREADS are crumbly cookies, more buttery than sweet. I pass a plate of them, along with the ripest fruit of the season and fruit knives. Dinner table conversation continues as each guest cuts his or her own fruit. It's a sociable end to a good dinner.

- ¾ cup (1½ sticks) butter, softened
- ½ cup sugar
- 1 large egg, separated
- 1¾ cups all-purpose flour
- ½ teaspoon ground cloves
- ⅛ teaspoon ground mace or nutmeg

In hot weather, substitute 1 teaspoon grated lemon zest for mace and cloves.

Preheat the oven to 325 degrees.

Cream butter in a large bowl. Add sugar and beat briefly to combine. Beat in egg yolk. Stir flour, cloves and mace or nutmeg into butter mixture (or mix with your hands).

Press into an ungreased 9-inch square baking pan. Brush lightly with beaten egg white.

Bake for 45 minutes, or until cake feels firm when pressed lightly. While still warm, cut into fingers about 1 inch wide and 3 inches long or into small squares. Cool, then remove from the pan.

Makes about 27 fingers or 24 squares. ~ **Serve with fresh fruit.**

Variation

Chocolate Chip Shortbread: Stir 1 cup semisweet chocolate mini chips into dough before pressing into the pan. Omit mace or nutmeg.

Peanut Butter-Oat Cookies

THE OAT AND PEANUT BUTTER partnership is delicious. Serve with a glass of cold milk.

- 1¼ cups peanut butter (any kind)
- ½ cup (1 stick) butter, softened
- 1 cup light or dark brown sugar
- 1 cup sugar
- 3 large eggs
- 1 teaspoon vanilla
- 1 cup all-purpose flour
- 1 teaspoon baking soda
- 3 cups quick-cooking or old-fashioned rolled oats

> These cookies can be dipped with a teaspoon or a tablespoon; decrease the cooking time if you make them small.

Preheat the oven to 350 degrees.

Beat peanut butter and butter together in a large bowl. Beat in brown sugar, then white sugar. Beat in eggs and vanilla. Stir in flour and baking soda until evenly mixed. Stir in oats.

Use a ¼-cup measure to dip dough onto an ungreased cookie sheet about 2½ inches apart (you can also use a large serving spoon, but you'll have to estimate the cooking time). Press each cookie mound firmly with the palm of your hand (these cookies don't spread much as they bake).

Bake for 20 minutes, or until cookies are tinged with darker brown on top. Remove to a cooling rack and cool completely.

Makes about 24 large cookies.

Variation

Chocolate Chip-Peanut Butter Cookies: Add 12 ounces semisweet chocolate mini chips to dough when you stir in oats.

Ultra-Easy Pound Cake

POUND CAKE ought to be easy: butter, sugar, eggs, flour. Beat it up, pour it in a pan. But there's so much that can go wrong: gummy valleys down the top, dry crumb, heavy texture. Why risk it? This recipe cheats a little, adding cream and fooling around with the "proper" pound-cake proportions. In exchange, you get perfect results every time. And the cake freezes beautifully. It's important to start with all ingredients at room temperature (about 70 degrees).

3 cups sugar
1 cup (2 sticks) butter, softened
6 large eggs
3 cups cake flour, sifted after measuring
1 cup heavy cream, whipping cream or sour cream
Powdered sugar, store-bought or homemade chocolate sauce or Lemon Sauce (opposite page)

Preheat oven to 325 degrees. Butter and flour a Bundt pan or kugelhopf pan. Set aside.

Beat sugar and butter together in a large bowl until well blended. Add eggs, one at a time, beating well after each addition. Stir flour into mixture alternately with cream, beginning and ending with flour.

Pour into the pan and bake for 1 hour, or until a toothpick comes out clean. Let cake cool on a rack for about 10 minutes, then turn out of the pan. If cake sticks, run a knife down a few of the pan "pleats" to loosen it.

Sprinkle with powdered sugar, serve with chocolate sauce, or toast slices under the broiler and serve them with Lemon Sauce.

Serves 12 to 16.

Lemon Sauce

SERVE OVER toasted pound cake or slices of angel food cake.

½ cup sugar
2 tablespoons cornstarch
1 cup water
3 tablespoons butter
Grated zest and juice of 1 lemon
⅛ teaspoon salt

Combine sugar, cornstarch and water in a small, heavy saucepan. Cook over medium-low heat, until mixture thickens and turns translucent.

Remove from the heat and stir in butter, lemon zest and juice and salt.

Makes about 1 cup, enough for about 6 servings.

Index